Praise for
Good Talk, Dad

"I love this book. It's no surprise the Geists have such broad appeal. I want them to be my dad and brother."

—Jim Gaffigan, author of *New York Times* bestseller *Dad Is Fat*

"Bill and Willie are the wittiest duo I know. Their stories are hilarious. Reading this book made me feel like I grew up a Geist!"

—Andy Cohen, host of Bravo's *Watch What Happens: Live* and author of *New York Times* bestseller *Most Talkative*

"Affectionate and raucous."

—*Chicago Tribune*

"[D]elightful...it is lovely, loving, and a must read."

—*Star-Ledger*

Lake
of the
Ozarks

Lake

of the

Ozarks

My Surreal Summers
in a Vanishing America

Bill Geist

GRAND CENTRAL
PUBLISHING

NEW YORK   BOSTON

Grand Central Publishing
Hachette Book Group
1290 Avenue of the Americas, New York, NY 10104
grandcentralpublishing.com
twitter.com/grandcentralpub

First edition: May 2019

Grand Central Publishing is a division of Hachette Book Group, Inc. The Grand Central Publishing name and logo is a trademark of Hachette Book Group, Inc.

The publisher is not responsible for websites (or their content) that are not owned by the publisher.

The Hachette Speakers Bureau provides a wide range of authors for speaking events. To find out more, go to www.hachettespeakersbureau.com or call (866) 376-6591.

Photo credits: page 35, created by G. Edwin Popkess; pages 92, 117, 125, Gina Chappell; page 123, Ina Kay Hibler Schlough. All other photographs courtesy of the author.

Library of Congress Cataloging-in-Publication Data

Names: Geist, William, author.
Title: Lake of the Ozarks : my surreal summers in a vanishing America / Bill Geist.
Description: New York : Grand Central Publishing, [2019]
Identifiers: LCCN 2018048035 | ISBN 9781538729809 (hardcover) | ISBN 9781538729816 (ebook)
Subjects: LCSH: Geist, William—Childhood and youth. | Ozarks, Lake of the, Region (Mo.)—Social life and customs—20th century. | Summer resorts—Missouri—Ozarks, Lake of the, Region—Anecdotes. | Teenage boys—Missouri—Biography. | Teenagers—Missouri—Social life and customs—20th century. | Missouri—Social life and customs—20th century—Anecdotes. | Summer employment—Missouri—Anecdotes. | Youth—Employment—Missouri—Anecdotes. | Coming of age.
Classification: LCC F472.O93 G45 2019 | DDC 977.8/493—dc23
LC record available at https://lccn.loc.gov/2018048035

ISBNs: 978-1-5387-2980-9 (hardcover), 978-1-5387-2981-6 (ebook), 978-1-5387-1637-3 (B&N.com signed edition)

Printed in the United States of America

LSC-C

10 9 8 7 6 5 4 3 2 1

*For Uncle Ed and Aunt Janet and all
members of the Arrowhead cast*

Laugh, and the world laughs with you;
Weep, and you weep alone;
For the sad old earth must borrow its mirth,
But has trouble enough of its own.

—Ella Wheeler Wilcox

Contents

Contents

Chapter One

The Drive Down /
Now and Then

*B*efore there was "tourism" or "leisure time"; before souvenir ashtrays became "camp" and "kitsch"; before the five-legged deer qualified as an "attraction"; and before today's colossal theme parks could even be imagined; there was "Beautiful

Lake of the Ozarks—Family Vacationland," where to this day the ashtrays remain devoid of irony.

Would going back to Lake of the Ozarks be a View-Master of fond memories or a series of electroshocks to the brain and stabs to the heart?

Arrowhead Lodge, where I worked for many summers during my high school and college years, was gone. Demolished in 2007. I hadn't been back to the lake since. Couldn't. Aunt Janet and Uncle Ed, my second set of parents, had owned the lodge and now they were gone too, along with the whole menagerie of wonderfully bizarre eccentrics drawn by their own peculiar circumstances to this remote, unlikely destination.

I didn't like to think about all of them and all of that, vaporized by the passage of time. It confused and angered me, time putting its jackboot on our necks as it stole our mothers and fathers, brothers and sisters, our favorite people and places, our health, our breath. What right does it have, death? When I meet it, I'll give it the finger. Best I can do.

I preferred remembering the lodge and the lake and the whole cast of characters just as they were. Or better. Or not at all. I wanted to drive up to the front door of the lodge and see a skinny, redheaded teenager sweeping the front walkway. Me. A half century later.

Arrowhead Lodge sat—and rather majestically, I'd say—on a wooded hilltop overlooking a three-mile stretch of glistening blue water edged in the vivid greenery of oak, hickory, ash, and black gum trees—with nary a man-made blemish.

Twenty thousand workers came to build Bagnell Dam, a 148-foot-high, half-mile-wide cement block plugging the Osage River.

A number of workers died during construction, giving their lives to provide us with power to light the darkness and totally awesome water-skiing.

The lake basin, cleared of all trees, structures, and people, living and dead, filled at about one and a half feet per day before topping out in 1931, 129 miles long with 1,375 miles of shoreline, more than California.

Arrowhead was built shortly thereafter, in 1935, from local timber and sandstone, with a large stone fireplace, wide-plank wooden walls, and rough-hewn furniture fashioned from hickory limbs and branches. It burned in 1950, but was quickly rebuilt and furnished to closely match the original.

Like nothing else built at the lake, Arrowhead Lodge looked like it belonged there. With forty-one guest rooms, a spacious lobby, and a restaurant that seated about 125 people, it was one of the largest and most luxurious hotels at the lake (albeit smaller and less luxurious than some Aspen ski homes today).

Speeding east on I-70 to catch the last plane from St. Louis to LaGuardia, I recalled old billboards showing euphoric speed-boaters, water-skiers, and anglers, all having the times of their lives at "Beautiful Lake of the Ozarks." To share in the bliss all one had to do was "Exit at Kingdom City," which I'd done so often in my life, but not for a very long time.

Should I?

Can't. Gotta get back home. Stuff to do.

But if not now, when? You're not getting any younger, pal.

I've never been able to make decisions. Give me anything, but don't give me a choice. Using my gray, midsized rental car as a kind of rolling Ouija board, I took my hands off the wheel. The car drifted slightly to the right, and so, guided by the paranormal, the hand of God, or uneven tire pressure, I took the Kingdom City exit.

Kingdom City, Missouri, falls short of its majestic name, just a truck stop, really. There used to be a folksy restaurant around here—the Chuck Wagon, was it? Or words to that effect— where you used to see truck drivers who appeared to be at once unquestionably male but, paradoxically, well into their third trimesters. They wore supportive, hubcap-sized silvery belt buckles, slung low, facing almost parallel to the ground.

There'd be farmers and hillbillies, too, missing a finger here, a few teeth there, but still managing to put away leaden platters of chicken fried steak, mashed potatoes, creamed corn, and biscuits—the whole of it smothered in gelatinous white gravy rapidly turning to stucco. Cholesterol? Trans fats? Nope, can't say I'd ever heard of 'em.

There were ashtrays on every table, for those who chose to go via the respiratory route rather than cardiovascular. No warning labels on the cigarette packs yet, but smokers *knew*. We already referred to them as "cancer sticks" and "coffin nails."

There were those little individual jukeboxes in every booth, featuring an eclectic mix of country, Motown, and rock 'n' roll: Elvis, Patsy Cline, the Temptations, as befitted this border state. You might think the music would have annoyed folks in the surrounding booths, but back then they just looked at it as free music. We didn't have "personal space" or "secondary smoke" yet either.

McDonald's and Taco Bell now squat there at the intersection of US 54 and I-70, which wasn't there yet either. No interstates at all back then, the wondrous system that allowed us to go very far, very fast, and not be slowed down by distractions, attractions, or interactions. America was now the same big green signs and exit ramps from the mountains to the prairies to the oceans white with foam and God bless it. I-70 in Missouri was the first section of the interstate system

With the coming of fast food, Kingdom City has yielded to bland conformity, but has not yet raised the greasy white flag of

5

surrender to the forces of "wellness." Didn't have "wellness" back then either, or "health care professionals." You just got sick and went to the doctor.

The old place had waitresses (not "waitstaff" or "servers") and glass glasses and breakable china. But no drive-throughs.

At McDonald's I tell the Big Talking Menu I'd like a Big Mac, medium fries, and a small Coke. "You mean the number three," said the Big Talking Menu, like I was a complete idiot for not knowing. I wanted to tell him that if I knew the numbers of all the McDonald's meals I'd shoot myself.

You could rightfully accuse me of being in denial, but what the hell? It's always worked for me. When my father died, then my mother, then my brother. It worked with Vietnam, I'm pretty sure. Haven't really thought about it. And now, with Parkinson's, I deny that, too, whenever I can.

It was at Arrowhead Lodge that I learned denial, trained by Uncle Ed and Aunt Janet not to root around for perceived faults in my upbringing, traumatic events, or current unpleasantries. And certainly not to *talk* about such things all the damned time as was becoming the fashion.

If I complained at all about anything around Aunt Janet, she'd look me straight in the eye and say: "You know what? Nobody really wants to hear about your problems." She'd known her share: her younger brother and my namesake—killed in World War II—two divorces, and a nearly fatal accident in an Istanbul taxi that left her with a chronic limp. She never talked about any of that. What good would it do?

And if ever I complained to Uncle Ed, a colonel in World War II, he'd dismiss it, saying, "See the chaplain."

Recalling that wholly insensitive remark made me laugh. I hooked a left and headed south toward the lake. I called Jody, my wife, to tell her of my change in plans. She said she understood, as she has for decades during her often inexplicable attachment to a roving correspondent who frequently doesn't know himself where he'll be the next day. Making plans and friends has not been easy. "Love you," I said, as though that were half enough.

US 54 snakes its way like Roto-Rooter down into the bowels of the Ozarks, passing through Fulton, Missouri, the town where Churchill delivered his historic "Iron Curtain" speech at Westminster College. I always thought Winston must have looked at the name of the school on the invitation, but not the location, when he accepted.

I switched on Sirius radio and dialed through the seven country channels, twelve sports, four rap, four conservative, two liberal...one of the remarkable new technological advances that sorts us out nicely for market. No fading out either, as Johnny Rabbitt on KXOK was wont to do as you entered these hilly nether regions in the old days. These days I tune to Classic Vinyl or Classic Rewind, music from back when I was young, or at least young-er, and very much alive. Jimi, Janis, James Brown, Clapton. Some of them—like some of me—gone now, yet when you crank the volume, you can still feel the beat of "Purple Haze," "Ball and Chain," and "I Got You (I Feel

Good)" vibrating in the armrests fifty years later. I hope they know that.

At Jefferson City, the old road crossed the mighty muddy Missouri River on a rattling claptrap bridge that looked and sounded like a dangerous old roller coaster hastily thrown up in the middle of the night by drunken carnies. The river was the sickly color of that thin, watery hot chocolate that grammar schools used to pawn off on patrol boys coming in from the cold.

I roll past the state capitol building, recalling the day I just may have been an accomplice in an act of official bribery. Then, past the former site of—Big Mo's, was it? Something like that—a steakhouse "Where the Meat's Bigger Than the Plate!" That was their pledge.

I have a sentimental attachment to Big Mo's (albeit not so strong that I can precisely recall its name). Dinner there was part of an incentive package that convinced a summer love to spend the night with me across the street at the Ramada Inn, also gone, but never to be forgotten.

The lake was forty-two miles south, undoubtedly less now on the new (to me) four-lane highway blasted straight and level through the solid-rock Ozark hills, a powerful reminder to Mother Nature of who's the friggin' boss around here. At present.

And these days, you can just put your car on cruise control and let 'er go. It doesn't really need us anymore. It knows how to get where it's going and can park itself, thanks. Our cars know when they're drifting out of their lanes and when they're about to impact other vehicles. For a few hundred bucks extra, some will call the EMTs when the airbags are deployed. It's only a matter of time until your crumpled wreckage can contact the nearest funeral parlor and order a nice FTD floral arrangement.

* * *

To a languid teenager sitting on the front steps waiting to see if another lightning bug might come by, the opportunity to spend a rip-roaring summer with my effervescent aunt and uncle at their cool resort seemed too good to be true. The speedboats! The bikinis!

Janet and Ed were quite different from my natural parents. My first memory of them is when they drove up to our little two-bedroom house in Champaign, Illinois, in a *QE2*-sized Packard.

Ed barged through the front door, larger and a good deal louder than life, flipping silver dollars in the air, which my older brother, David, and I dove to catch before they hit the floor.

Janet wore a long elegant winter coat that must have cost the lives of an entire company of minks. (Just their luck being born into a species rated "of least concern" by animal rights groups.) Their coats for hers. She wore one of the most striking in her collection, a herringbone patterned number with alternating stripes of black, brown, and white pelts.

These were big shots! They'd recently returned from a cruise, as always, and told us tales of exotic, far-off lands as we sat rapt.

When Ed and Janet arrived, it was always like the circus coming to town. I remember attending a college football game with Ed where he pulled out a wad of hundred-dollar bills, sneaked a few to me, and we commenced to bet on every play. "I'll bet you a Benjamin they get a first down," he'd say loudly. The winner would snatch the two hundreds and we were on to the next play. "Bet you a hundred they pass." My friends were astounded—not to mention scores of those around us who stood and pointed at the two high-rollers making big bets on small things.

Everything changed when they were around. They drank, they laughed, they carried on. My mom and dad, Marge and Russ, were Mennonites by comparison.

Mom and Dad never left the U.S. Apart from a couple of trips to Arrowhead Lodge, I don't recall them traveling outside the state of Illinois.

My mom was fond of saying: "Little boats don't go far from shore"—referring to distance and aspiration.

She wore a red coat with a faux fur collar, which she referred to as her "Republican cloth coat," a phrase Richard Nixon used to describe his wife's outerwear in response to allegations he was lavishly spending campaign funds on Pat and himself.

It seemed to me my mom could do anything and everything. She sewed, upholstered furniture, wallpapered and painted the house, and with a little muscle power from my dad, built a brick patio. She typed college term papers for me and turned into a full-blown accountant at her sister's CPA firm during tax season. All this in addition to cooking, shopping, washing dishes and clothes, cleaning the house and the myriad of unrelenting, thankless tasks that fell to women of the era. I always said she could have easily run General Motors if she'd had the chance. She was smart, organized, and energetic. She always put others' needs and wants ahead of her own. Our kids loved Grandma Marge and though she's been gone for many years now they still speak of her most fondly and often. I think of her and wish I could have been much nicer.

But despite all of her great qualities and talents, she somehow exuded a sense of low self-esteem and low expectations. Notre Dame would never ask her to give fiery win-one-for-the-Gipper half-time pep talks, let's put it that way.

This must have come from having an older sister who was salutatorian of a university class of thousands, a talented athlete and violinist, a CPA, and a pilot, among her other accomplishments. I always say, "Aunt Betty received only one B the whole time she was in college...and so did I."

My older brother, David, who gave a commencement address on stage between two beautiful palms, played the coronet in dance band, won several music awards, was a mainstay of various student groups, and even had his own local radio show, somehow absorbed Mom's message. Later he would say he always suffered a feeling of inferiority because his friends belonged to the country club.

But during night ceremonies at Boy Scout camp *he* was the guy in full Indian regalia standing on a burning platform high in the treetops. "That's my big brother!" I was the second-class Scout afraid to jump in the swimming pool.

I dealt with the inferiority thing by hanging out with kids who didn't belong to the country club and would have been kicked out if they had. They were lots more fun. I'm a sucker for fun. They were not your tiptop students. A couple of them were greasers who drove hot rods. Some siphoned gas from cars on the street. One was elected to high office in our class. Another grew up to be far and away the wealthiest person in town. My father frequently cautioned: "If you keep hanging around with those guys you'll wind up in jail." I did, too, charged with underage drinking (beer).

We didn't have money. My dad was a high school shop teacher, who taught printing and photography. He always had a little black ink under his fingernails. He wore inexpensive rubber-soled shoes because he was on his feet all day.

Dad commuted one mile to and from work in an old but low-mileage green Chevrolet that he'd inherited from his dad, who purchased it, became ill, and put it in the garage. Better that than our hulking, black '49 Buick Roadmaster. Riding in that, if I saw a cute girl, I'd slide down in the passenger seat until my head was below window level. You just could not have a big, old black car in your driveway in the fifties.

Thanks to Mom's budgeting acumen, we had a nice house, nice clothes, and even a nice car once we traded in the '49 Buick for a '59 with long fins I feared would impale gas station attendants. (FYI, a gas station attendant was a guy who filled your gas tank, checked your oil, coolant and battery fluids, and tire pressure.) But those old gas stations did not sell hats and T-shirts, sixty-two different candy bars, and fifty-seven kinds of refrigerated beverages, including twenty brands of bottled water. There were no "brands" of water, only God's. It was free. I know. Sounds crazy.

I didn't really notice that we never took vacations. In summers, to supplement his teacher's salary, Dad operated a Linotype machine, which turned molten metal into headlines, at the Alton, Illinois, *Telegraph* newspaper. We stayed in the searing attic of my grandparents' brick bungalow in Belleville, Illinois, where they kept the thermostat on "Bake."

Janet and Ed lived in nearby East St. Louis, in what was then, believe it or not, a ritzy neighborhood. Uncle Ed was a big shot in the Shriners. He took me to the Shrine Circus where we had VIP seats. The star of the show was a cowpoke named Red Ryder, who I later met in person back at Ed's house. My uncle Ed *knew* Red Ryder, who never achieved the status of Gene Autry or Roy Rogers, but was big back then, he and his sidekick, Little Beaver.

In Belleville, I was the lone kid in the neighborhood and out of necessity became inventive at creating solitaire sports. I played baseball like other kids do, except I was the only player on both teams. I'd fire a tennis ball off the foundation of the house, chase the ball, and make the throw to first base— a large tree. I was usually Stan "The Man" Musial while at the same time Cardinals sportscaster Harry Caray.

"Who are you talking to out there?" my grandmother would yell from the kitchen window.

I would go on to invent Garage Ball, which involved a garage (a precursor to the domed stadium), a bat, and a tennis ball and a lot of tricky ricocheting.

I learned to entertain myself. Ofttimes these days I'll be walking with someone and start chuckling. "What's funny?" they'll ask. "Oh, nothing," I'll reply, smiling.

In Vietnam I invented Fan Ball in which a small group of soldiers stands in a circle beneath a high-speed ceiling fan. A wet, muddy tennis ball (not easy to find in the remote jungles of Southeast Asia) is tossed into the swirling blades and our men in uniform try to catch it. This resulted in bloody noses—one treated by army medics—and reprimands from the sergeant. Tricky, since I outranked him.

Dad never talked much. I figured he'd had enough interaction with kids (much of it unpleasant) during the day. He once asked me at the dinner table: "Do you say everything that comes to your mind?" I was just trying to liven up this taciturn bunch.

Mom talked incessantly—making an effort to fill the unnatural void. She ended all her sentences with an "and a" or a "but a," thereby holding the floor.

My parents graduated college with degrees in journalism and bought a small country newspaper, the *Fisher Reporter*. Those were Depression times. Mom traded newspaper ads for groceries, and Dad spent much of his time under the press with wrenches, trying to make it run.

They eventually gave up on that and moved to Champaign, where they opened Campus Printers. When it burned to the ground, he became a schoolteacher.

He had few pleasures. He gave up smoking and drinking before my time, plus one of his great loves, flying. Too expensive. Dad would take me to a small local airport and we'd taxi around on the ground in a little yellow Piper J-3 Cub with the doors open.

I think my mother feared he'd crash. His younger brother, Bill, died at age twenty in a B-17 Flying Fortress bomber in World War II, just ten days before the end of the war and two weeks before I was born and named after him: William Everett Geist. I don't think anyone in the family was ever quite the same. No one ever talked about him. Too painful. I got to know a little about him when I was given a small suitcase of his things, including a diary and some yearbooks signed by many friends who said they always had fun when he was around. There was also a photograph of my grandparents receiving some sort of Gold Star certificate as they looked away with thousand-mile stares.

He seemed a lot like me except he was a really good tennis player. He wrote witty articles for the college newspaper. At times, I feel like I'm carrying the flag for Uncle Bill. Or trying.

My mother's reaction to most everything was to warn of its inherent dangers. I think that may be a reason I grew up to become a professional observer. No matter what the activity you could usually find me on the sidelines . . . making observations.

Although our first house was tiny and our second one small, there was Dad's piano in the corner of the living room. He played almost every evening after dinner, much of the time with his eyes closed, off in his own world. So glad he still had that. (He could play by heart any song anyone could think of, which put him at the center of party sing-alongs.)

Then he'd head downstairs to his darkroom, where he shut the door so light couldn't get in to ruin his film and his prints. Of course, we couldn't get in either. But when we passed the door we could hear jazz on his radio. I can still hear strains of Fats Waller singing "Ain't Misbehavin'."

* * *

The nice thing about growing up in Champaign was that the rest of the world was so fascinating. There was no ocean for at least a thousand miles. No mountains, no hills, even. I didn't see the ocean until I was twenty, on my first trip out of the country, to Acapulco, with Janet and Ed as a matter of fact. There was no airport in Acapulco then. They met me in Mexico City in a gold Cadillac, where we were accosted by street urchins asking for handouts. Ed pointed at me and said: "*Mucho dinero!*" and they rushed me.

There were no real highways either. We drove on narrow roads up and down the steep hills with no guardrails, Ed making stops so kids could stick large iguanas in the window and ask if I'd like to buy one.

16

We arrived at Acapulco at night. "What's that sound?" I asked.

"Waves," they explained.

We went deep-sea fishing and caught eight-foot sailfish that leaped high in the air, twisting and turning dramatically before splashdowns.

Back home we didn't even have lakes. My first fishing trip was to a pond created when dirt was scooped out to build an overpass. It was stocked with that least desirable and totally-not-a-real-game-fish: carp. Some enterprising fellows charged a couple of bucks to fish there and although we didn't catch anything they gave us a stringer of big ugly ones for photographs, taken before my dad buried them in the garden as fertilizer.

Didn't have a passport until I was forty. Hadn't seen a mountain yet.

Champaign was provincial. How provincial? Well, our high school foreign exchange student was from America. Hawaii. Who knew?

To me, Lake of the Ozarks seemed like an exotic locale. Although "exotic" may be a stretch. Angkor Wat is exotic.

* * *

Back in the sixties this stretch from Jeff City to the lake wasn't so quick and easy. No microwaving an instant vacation back then. Tourists found themselves trying to navigate an unwelcoming, winding, two-lane road, with double-yellow, no-passing center stripes nearly all the way to the lake, as it leaped and twisted this way and that through the Ozark hills, like a bull at the Camdenton Rodeo trying to buck a cowpoke. It was almost as if they didn't really want people to come.

Tires picked up rocks that click-clack-clickity-clacked for many a mile before kicking back into the grills and windshields of cars behind. We didn't have rocks and hills back home in central Illinois, just flat, black soil laid out in neat, one-mile squares.

Their white knuckles gripping the steering wheels, newcomers drove slowly, trailing caravans of cars behind them. Despite the double yellow lines, some frustrated drivers took their chances at Miller's Flats, causing many a shit-your-pants near misses and the occasional head-on. Officials put the twisted wreckages in front of the local high school as a warning to teens, but stopped when the grounds took on the look of a salvage yard.

No airbags back then and people complained that those new seat belts were uncomfortable to sit on. (I considered wearing seat belts an insult to the driver.) There's a sharp, twenty-five-mile-per-hour curve where I rolled my VW Beetle with no seat belts and no injuries. (Note to motorists: When signs in Missouri say it's a twenty-five-mile-per-hour curve they mean it.) My four passengers were crammed so tightly into my small car there was no space for them to be thrown. Built of heavier gauge steel in those days, the car kept its shape.

You'd go by unpainted barns with rusty corrugated tin roofs

and billboards for fertilizer next to those for small resort motels and beauty shops (Kathy's Kut-n-Kurl).

Finally, the old road passed the El-Donna Motel in Eldon, Missouri, then by a roadside monument that bore this encouraging message carved in stone: "Gateway—Lake of the Ozarks."

Indeed it was. There were harbingers of what was to come in the family vacationland ahead. If you were thinking Cape Cod you'd come to the wrong place. If, however, you enjoyed watching monkeys drive small cars—and who doesn't?—this was the place for you.

Monkeys driving little cars! Right here at Tom's Monkey Jungle. And so much more!

Would you ever have imagined when you woke up that morning you'd see a coatimundi? Me neither. How about a herd of white deer from India or China or someplace like that? Or pygmy skunks and guinea pigs?

You could pet the monkeys, hold them, and, if you got completely carried away, buy one. The ASPCA didn't really have a strong foothold in the area. Tom said he didn't aggressively push monkey sales. They were more of an impulse purchase.

Monkeys in Eldon! You had to hand it to Tom. Way out there on a two-lane road in rural Missouri, he probably could have gotten away with a raccoon and two spray-painted squirrels.

Next stop: Max Allen's Reptile Gardens, exhibiting poisonous reptiles, Oh, goody. Gila monsters, and George, a 250-pound tortoise from the Galápagos. (Is that down by Cape Girardeau?) "Honey, get a picture of little Jimmy riding the big turtle." If you're of a certain age, you probably have just such a photograph (black and white or yellowed) showing an unsmiling you with something along the lines of a really big turtle.

Max had monkeys and apes too. And gators and seals—in Eldon! Awesome, Max! (Make that "Good going, Max!" We weren't using "awesome" yet.)

Driving ever dam-ward, intrepid vacationers next pulled off the road at the Ozark Deer Farm, which was pretty nice but lacked that certain . . . je ne sais quoi . . . of the Monkey Jungle and the Reptile Gardens. Although, the five-legged deer was nothing to sneeze at.

After Indian Burial Cave lay Guns and Ammo, my last landmark before the dam, where we used to buy .22 longs to sink beer cans in a pond behind the lodge.

Just beyond it, you could catch that first exhilarating glimpse—There! Through those trees!—of the sparkling blue lake, the goal of this long, winding, twisting, turning journey. Lake of the Ozarks—Midwestern Shangri-la—where I learned to be a man, a certain kind of man.

Chapter Two

The Strip

*E*xcitement mounted as vacationers coasted downhill between a tall rock cut-through, then rolled right across the very top of mighty Bagnell Dam.

Nothing could have prepared them for what they were about to encounter on the other side, a raucous carnival midway, an ambush of gaudy signs and loudspeakers and young girls passing out flyers hawking "Helicopter Tours!," "Seaplane Rides!," "50 mph Speedboat Thrill Rides!," "Spectacular Sightseeing Tours," and ersatz Mississippi River–style paddleboat rides offering "the finest tours—guaranteed."

Adult male tourists looked the part, morphing from the office stage to vacation stage, yet to shed their shiny black leather shoes and ankle-length black socks, but donning shorts, short-sleeved shirts (tucked in), and maybe a souvenir straw hat with tiny beer cans attached. And, of course, Instamatics around their necks.

21

They never knew what hit them. The barkers did everything but shoot out their tires. "Daddy! Stop! Stop! Can we go on a boat ride? Can we? Can we? Pleeease?!"

Most of the families were frugal, middle-class Midwesterners, the parents having grown up in the Depression, wearing hand-me-downs, dining on beanie-weenie casseroles and "meat" loaf that was 90 percent oatmeal. The parents played cards (0 dollars) and ate popcorn (25 cents for four) for entertainment on Saturday nights (add 40 cents for four Cokes, 20 cents for Pepsis). They rarely or never went out to restaurants. They lived in small homes, two kids to a bedroom, one bath, and drove used cars. Take my family, for example.

But the kids didn't really want a grim history lesson or an economic feasibility study at the moment. And up against this army of barkers, what chance did Mom and Dad really have? Okay, Dad rented the goddamned speedboat—at fifty dollars an hour!—piloting the vessel over the bounding waves as the kids shrieked with joy and Mom grimaced at the image in her head: standing in a grocery store checkout lane pushing an empty shopping cart.

Souvenir shops drew them in with a dazzling array of "Lake of the Ozarks" shot glasses, salt-and-pepper shakers, coffee mugs, ashtrays, decorative wall plates, and black velvet pillowcases festooned with neon-colored likenesses of Bagnell Dam. There were miniature license plates with a variety of first names stamped on them. If your name was Bob or John, you were in good shape. Conversely, if it was, say, something like Verlin, it would be a long day of spinning the little racks.

There were wallets with likenesses of the dam or Fabian glued on, foot-long "hillbilly" cigars, rubber bloody severed hands, and plastic vomit. A classic. And a sign that read "Electric Toilet Tissue" but provided no further product information.

Here in the land of the Osage, there were scads of Native American–related (if distantly) novelties: rubber tomahawks, spears, tom-toms, felt moccasins, and belts with "Lake of the Ozarks" emblazoned in colorful plastic beads and "Made in Japan" stamped on the back. I imagined bewildered assembly line workers in Yokohama shaking their heads in wonder at all this.

Fireworks. I always loaded up with cherry bombs at five cents a pop then sold them back home for a quarter.

Watching over it all was a thirty-foot-tall fiberglass individual dressed like a hillbilly but with the face of Alfred E. Neuman

There were bumper cars, of course, and one of my favorites, Skee-Ball, where the skillful roller could "Win Valuable Prizes," some more than others. If you spent ten dollars playing the game, you'd almost certainly have enough prize points to walk away a winner with, say, a small plastic pocket comb. The prize counter prominently displayed the good stuff, like life-sized stuffed panda bears, which, if you were a decent player, would probably wind up costing you...oh...around two hundred dollars.

Seeing as how this was the Ozarks and all, there was Hillbilly Golf and lots of hillbilly-themed souvenirs, too, like corncob pipes and floppy, cone-shaped hillbilly hats—and rare mementos I've never seen anywhere else. Take, for example, a cedar plaque to hang outside your bathroom door that poses the question: "Who's on the Pot?" If it was Dad, he'd hang "Pa" on the plaque. There were also tags for "Sis," "Brother," and "Ma." I would have liked more information.

Vacation apparel shops sold T-shirts with amusing messages like "I'm with Stupid" (rather than today's snappy "F-You" tees that discriminating shoppers can find on, say, the Jersey Shore).

There was a "ski" lift to the top of a small hill—and back. It would have been more exciting if hillbillies were mountain-billies. But, alas, absent mountains and skiing, this attraction didn't last long.

Dogpatch was something of a theme park all its own, a big souvenir store with a re-creation of a hillbilly town in back, plus Old Bob's Cabin, a hillbilly jail, an animated graveyard with protruding, wiggling toes, and an outhouse occupied by a seated mechanical man who yelled when someone opened the door: "Hey, get outta here! Can't you see I'm on the pot?" Ha! Out front was a mule the kids could ride and a real, live caged lion! The lion wasn't really in keeping with the overall theme but was a helluva stand-alone attraction.

My favorite was the completely mystifying Mystery Spot, also known as Phantom Acres, where—don't ask me how—

water appeared to flow uphill—up! hill—and people stood at forty-five-degree angles to the floor.

* * *

I fell in love with all this and over time became something of a connoisseur, an aficionado of the tacky and outrageous, i.e., my America. Ultimately this became my beat as a newspaper reporter and TV correspondent. I wrote about a boom in plastic pink flamingos and how the fancier could tell a Chicago plastic flamingo from the species manufactured in Massachusetts. I identified the inventor of Twinkies who not even the Hostess corporation knew about. I had an exclusive on a suspected terrorist attack at McDonald's corporate headquarters. A leather case left momentarily in the lobby was robotically removed by an overeager suburban bomb squad and exploded in a nearby field. It was Ronald McDonald's makeup kit.

I covered the Caesars Palace twenty-fifth anniversary gala in Vegas for the *Tribune*. Liberace and Donald Trump for the *Times*, Graceland and sofa-sized art for CBS.

I mean, I was *there*...at WrestleMania I. And I'm not saying this makes me better than you, but I know, *personally*, Ron Popeil, inventor of the Popeil's Pocket Fisherman. I interviewed him at his home in the Hollywood Hills for CBS. I own his Egg Scrambler, which scrambles eggs *inside* their shells. (Why ask why?) I have in my office the Popeil's Sit-On Trash

Compactor (in avocado, so it goes with everything): Remove top. Place trash in masher. Sit on top. Trash is mashed.

At first, I was astonished that visitors to Lake of the Ozarks were actually purchasing Bagnell Dam salt-and-peppers and toothpick holders.

But I found myself collecting such items, thinking (thinking?) that Americans would one day become too sophisticated for such tacky mementos and that such things would disappear altogether.

I had this crazy idea, see, that mankind was *evolving*. That the human race was becoming better educated, more intelligent, more sophisticated. And get this! That television would play a key role in the process, by exposing the masses to culture: opera, ballet, symphony orchestras, theater, classic films, fine art exhibits, and the like.

Has anyone ever been so terribly, terribly wrong?

There's a lot of money to be made betting against me. I advised the author of *Chaos* that I wasn't at all sure there was a mass audience for a physics book. It was atop the bestseller lists for a year.

An executive at CBS told me about the network's idea for a new reality show called *Survivor*. After he explained it to me I told him I thought it was one of the stupidest ideas I'd ever heard. It's heading into its thirty-eighth season.

Chapter Three

The Tourist Trappers

*W*ho dreamed up all this stuff anyhow? No one completely normal. Not that I've come across.

Larry Albright was one. He and other great minds of the midway met for coffee at the lodge—irregularly, as befitted this group of irregulars; these were gatherings of local entrepreneurs who wanted to keep abreast of the latest developments in the burgeoning tourist trap industry—and, when possible, steal each other's ideas.

When Uncle Ed somehow managed to procure a liquor license, the get-togethers moved downstairs to the new Pow Wow Pub, with Bloody Marys subbing for coffee. It became something of a Rotary Club for the functioning alcoholic.

Several of these men were World War II veterans who'd returned home and found themselves ill suited for corporate desk jobs: "Paper pushing and kissing ass," as one put it. Lake of the Ozarks was about as far from that as they could get; about as far from anything, come to think of it. In that time of conformity and the Organization Man, these guys were having none of it.

They were people who lived by their own rules. They may very well have been some rare undiscovered strain of do-your-own-thing rural beatniks or hippies and not known it. A couple of them probably had PTSD but that hadn't been invented yet. They were old school and probably wouldn't have sought treatment for anything less than a missing arm.

Living by your own rules can make life more interesting and more fun, but at times way more difficult than going with the soothing flow.

I was already showing signs of a predisposition toward their philosophy of life when I met them.

As an elementary school student, I sat in the hall a lot. Or the principal's office. I was made to stay after school to clean erasers with the janitor. (Is it too late for me to sue the school district or the chalk industry for exposing me to Hazardous Dust Inhalation [HDI]?) In junior high, after-school detention became a regular part of my school day. There I hobnobbed with Edison Junior High's all-stars of disruption.

I recently found one of those wallet-sized photos, the ones we used to trade in school, of my homeroom teacher in ninth grade, Barbara Lee Schemmel. She wrote on the back: "To the most amusing troublemaker in 9-3."

She called me a "disrupter." These days, start-ups in Silicon Valley proudly call themselves "disrupters" and make billions of dollars disrupting. It's become a good thing, a questioning of the old, rusty, worn-out, and outdated ways of thinking about and doing things. It's taken decades but I'm finally flattered.

* * *

Larry Albright was the acknowledged "Souvenir King" of the Lake of the Ozarks. And that was saying a mouthful.

Next to him at one morning get-together was a lesser light, Al Huber, who had a myriad of micro-marketing schemes but none that were going to vault him into the Forbes 500. Still, the group gave him his due. He was trying.

Conversely, there was Walt Tietmeyer, the mastermind of Dogpatch, that Ozark village replicated on the strip.

Al Lechner was much admired by the others for having "a true gift" for attracting vacationers. Al brought the popular Phantom Acres to the strip, later renaming it the Mystery Spot, where gravity was reversed and water flowed uphill.

Most people, including me, thought these guys were all nuts.

The difference was, I liked them that way. And have never stopped. It took years—until quite recently, actually—for me to recognize the impact those summers at Lake of the Ozarks had on me. I can now trace the focus of practically my entire career back to this brand of characters and to my admittedly odd attraction to them.

I later sought them out in the bland beige-ness of the suburbs as a columnist for the *Chicago Tribune*—and found them too: nonconforming misfits who refused to mow their lawns to the required length, rebels who flagrantly left their garage doors open in violation of local ordinances, painted their houses in unapproved hues; or placed illicit pink plastic flamingos in their front yards, not only because they were attractive, but sometimes just to flaunt their independence, to let their freak flamingos fly.

Give me a renegade eccentric over a drab, rule-abiding conformist every time. I liked one-of-a-kind people who thought for themselves, sometimes inspired by genius, at other times by clinical insanity. At least they were alive. It made me think I was too.

I discovered the inventor of Twinkies. Okay, he wasn't Dr. Jonas Salk, but had it not been for my reportage, James Dewar would never have had an obituary in the *New York Times*.

I wrote about a man who claimed alien beings were going to land in a spaceship (with a Dewar's scotch ad painted on its side) in a remote suburban field to deliver the formula for powdered gasoline. Hundreds of people showed up, although the spaceship did not. The U.S. attorney's office charged the man

31

with running a scam; I charged the U.S. attorney with trying to protect the essentially unprotectable stupid idiots among us.

I figured if these unique human specimens could be found in the suburbs they could be found anywhere.

In New York if I didn't have an aberrant subject for a column, I could just take a walk around the block. At CBS I followed their trails to the ends of the earth: Maine to California, Washington to Florida, Japan, Korea, France, Norway, Great Britain, Bermuda, the Virgin Islands, Canada.

In Bithlo, Florida, it was Robert Hart, who invented figure-eight school-bus racing. What a concept! "I won't brake 'til I see God," one driver told me. Hart's only bow to sanity: no students on the buses during races. Yet.

In Colorado, it was a couple of hard-luck entrepreneurs who finally hit it big by sucking unwanted prairie dogs out of their holes with an old sewer vacuum truck, then selling them through some sort of prairie dog broker to pet shops in Tokyo, which charged as much as $900 per pair.

In Whalan, Minnesota (population: 62), local folk had always wanted to have a parade but couldn't figure out a way to do it in a town less than two blocks long. It would be over before it began. David Harrenstein moved to the little town with a big idea: the "stand-still parade," wherein the color guard, the grand marshal waving from a red convertible, marching bands, floats, horseback riders, and fire trucks (from other towns since Whalan didn't have any) stood still when the parade started and the crowd *walked around* the parade.

Hanlontown, Iowa, celebrated the day the sun set in the middle of the railroad tracks. (That was a close one. I'd flown halfway across the country and the clouds didn't lift 'til ten minutes before sunset.)

Nederland, Colorado, held Frozen Dead Guy Days. Thousands show up every year now to celebrate a young man from Norway who kept his deceased grandfather, Bredo, packed in dry ice in a backyard shed. Visitors pay to see the burial spot if not Grandpa Bredo himself—too much ice piled on him. He's still there, although one neighbor says Bredo may have experienced some freezer burn over the years.

I profiled Judge Roy Hofheinz, a larger-than-life Texan who owned the Colt .45s (now the Astros) baseball team. He became so annoyed at the steam-bath climate and the large attack mosquitoes at the games, that he enclosed and air-conditioned a vast expanse of the Texas plains, the Houston Astrodome, the world's first domed stadium. Outrageous idea back then.

And Edward Bernays, "the Father of Public Relations." You know how ophthalmologists said you were supposed to have a light on in the room when you watched TV? Well, it wasn't ophthalmologists who said it. It was Bernays, who made that up when TVs hit the market and he was working for GE lightbulbs. Bernays was a pioneer of professional prevarication, there at the birth of this era of high-grade premium, professional, pervasive bullshit we now find ourselves buried in.

Suffice it to say, then, that I had Donald Trump pegged from the moment we met when I was writing a *New York Times*

Magazine cover story on him way back in 1984. Back then I found him most amusing. "Oh, Donald lies a great deal," said world-renowned architect Philip Johnson, who was designing a castle (with a moat and a drawbridge) for Trump, "but usually it's not about anything terribly important."

Alas!

For me, it was something as goofy as the pro wrestling boom in the seventies that made me see just how far along we'd sped down bullshit highway. How had *wrestling* become so hugely popular when it was so obviously fake? People didn't care. (Donald is a member of the World Wrestling Entertainment Hall of Fame and president of the United States.)

Uncle Ed was considered something of a blowhard in his day but that was back when there was still shame, embarrassment, and the like. These days he'd be small potatoes, but he taught me by example the ways of the new world.

I gave the commencement address a few years ago at the University of Illinois, where students knew the aroma of actual bullshit as it occasionally wafted through campus from nearby farms. But I sounded the alarm for them to be aware of virulent new strains of odious but odorless bullshit and to watch for it everywhere they stepped.

Sophisticated bullshit, based on neuroscience and algorithms. Advertising and marketing campaigns that know what you want before you do. Dangerous military bullshit that convinces you war is exciting and will make a hero out of you. Costly bullshit that parts you with your money, while promising to "get the IRS off your back." Fearmongering political bull-shit. Pill pushers on TV ("may cause internal bleeding or death" but it might not) and personal injury lawyers, formerly known as ambulance chasers: "Have you been head-on'd, T-boned, rear-ended? Or maybe you've tripped on someone's sidewalk?" Talk radio and TV bullshitters who tell you that their fake news is the real news and that the real news is fake news...and so on.

To ward off today's torrential bullshit you need the premium bullshit protection package. Earplugs to keep it out of your head and a Slomin's security alarm system to keep it out of your home.

The summer I was Arrowhead's pool attendant I received my first lesson in commercial embellishment.

Ours was the oldest swimming pool on the lake—circa 1948—with an antiquated filter system that required the continual adding of fresh water. There was no heater. The water came from a four-hundred-foot well; those of you who've tiptoed into Lake Superior have a good idea of just how cold the pool water was. The sound of a guest diving in went something like this:

Splash!

"Aieeeeeeee!!! Jesus Christ! Did some jackass turn off the heater?"

"It's solar heated," I'd reply, which made it sound like we had some advanced enviro-friendly eco-heating system. Except we didn't have enviro or eco anything back then.

We had the sun, which did warm the water a few degrees in the days and weeks after the icy water was added.

"Give it a few minutes," I'd say, lying. Make that "fibbing."

I vacuumed the bottom of the pool, then skimmed the surface for leaves, drowned squirrels, and the occasional baby turd. Actually, the lone "baby turd" turned out to be a Baby Ruth candy bar Pete had tossed in to startle me, and it did. You may have seen this in the movie *Caddyshack*, but Pete Havely, my coworker, had conceived the concept decades earlier.

I hosed down the concrete deck around the pool every morning and picked up empty beer bottles and cigarette butts. And every day I raked the three-foot-wide strip of sand around two sides of the pool, referred to as a "sand beach" in our brochure.

"*This* is what you call a sand beach?" disgruntled guests would yell at me.

If guests complained too much or too loudly within earshot of Aunt Janet, she became very defensive, getting up in their faces.

The colorful brochure touted other imagined amenities such as "water-skiing instructor," which always created a moment of panic when someone asked for a lesson, because there were no skis, no boat, and no instructor. If things got ugly, we'd use Ed's speedboat and, although I was a piss-poor once-a-year skier who had never stayed up on one ski, I instructed on a couple of occasions. "Keep the tips up...tips together...don't stand up...let the boat pull you up...bend your knees...don't lean too far forward...or backward...let go of the rope when you fall...let go of the rope...for chrissake let go of the rope!"

* * *

Larry Albright was considered something of a genius amongst tourist trappers. Indeed, he wore his hair in an explosive Einstein cut. He was, if I may say so, on the rather dumpy and disheveled side in terms of physique and apparel choices. Not to mention said apparel was always covered with cat hair. He drove a very used (cars were yet to be "pre-owned"), goldenish Cadillac with a leatherette "Landau" top, once part of the luxury package but was now peeling in an unsightly manner.

Larry lived beneath his souvenir empire in two rooms he shared with his fifty cats. Five-oh. He built them an outdoor playground where they could snooze, climb carpeted poles, swat cat toys, and snooze. They lived on prime lakefront property but never swam. When he held them they ungratefully peed on his shirt. This did not stop him from wearing the shirt time and again.

I loved hearing Larry's tales, frequently tall, and he loved telling them, never quite the same way twice. Many tired of this. Not me, which was probably why it was me he invited for dinner. He plucked an orange-and-white long-haired feline from a pot and began to cook. When I told Aunt Janet about Larry's dinner invitation, she remarked, "Eat first."

Larry told of his career in the restaurant business. His first two forays ended somewhat tragically, somewhat not, both restaurants burning to the ground, fully insured, after they'd closed for the season.

"Thank God," Larry said, "no one was killed."

"It's a miracle," I replied.

His third culinary venture went belly up amidst scurrilous, unsubstantiated rumors started by a competitor that Larry was using roadkill in his entrées. Another competitor was said to have gone so far as to charge that he had seen traces of the Goodyear imprint on Larry's "flank steak." Larry recalled sitting on the floor in the middle of the empty restaurant taking long swigs from a bottle of cheap bourbon, throwing bottles of French dressing against the walls, and muttering repeatedly, "This has got to stop."

"But I couldn't trust myself to stop," he explained. "I wound up taking the drastic measure of sawing one leg off of each table in the restaurant, so I could never open another one."

A big question remains open to this day.

Larry has a peg leg.

Did he... by any chance... you know?

Al Huber had big ideas for pulling customers off the highway to his small restaurant on the strip.

"What I'm gonna do," he whispered confidentially, "is put

dirt from every state in the union in the flower box outside the front door."

His eyes widened and he nodded as if to say, "Is that great or what?"

"That ought to really bring 'em in, Al," Pete commented.

"You prob'ly oughta put up some sort of sign to let people know what they're lookin' at," a fellow tourist trapper suggested helpfully. Noted.

Al confessed that he was still about twenty-two states short. "Do you think anyone would notice if you put a bunch more Missouri dirt on the bottom?" another trapper asked.

The flower box dirt medley was just for openers. Al had a million of 'em. "I'm gonna take frozen pies and put 'em in the oven about four in the morning, see, and take 'em out and sniff 'em like they're real home-baked pies." Pete and I nodded our approval.

Al had noticed there was no beach at the lake, since creating sand required eons of pounding surf, not thirty years of gently lapping lake water. So he trucked in a couple tons, dumped it on shore, and voilà! Al Huber's Play-a-Day Beach. "And that's not all! I'm gonna row children out in the cove in the afternoon," he explained enthusiastically, "and read them fairy tales."

Play-a-Day hung on for about ten years, not a bad run in the mercurial tourism trade.

Al Lechner owned the most popular attraction on the strip: The Mystery Spot (or Phantom Acres). You know, the place where, inexplicably, gravity was reversed. Science held no answers. Al explained that a meteorite plummeted to earth, landing on the amusement strip, a mile south of the dam, next door to Dogpatch, reversing gravity and leaving just enough room for parking. No one was injured. I don't know if this was the same meteorite that wiped out the dinosaurs or not.

Al and a partner, Lee Mace, originator of the popular Ozark Opry show, leased Indian Burial Cave where business picked up when Lee touted the cave to his sold-out audiences. And even more so when Indian bones began poking out of the ground near the cave's ticket booth.

An idea was floated for an underwater mermaid show, which, lo and behold, actually happened. Mermaids in the Ozarks! Attractive young women in mermaid suits swam underwater in a huge aquarium, taking hits of oxygen from a hookah to avoid drowning.

A few wheeler-dealers had bigger ideas. They bought cheap land on uninhabited Shawnee Bend directly across the lake from the lodge. Shawnee was only about a mile by boat but eighty miles or more by car and no roads to get there. The property was almost worthless...unless...a bridge was built. And of course it was.

Tex Varner and his wife, Hope, were virtuosos. Didn't see much of Tex after his murder conviction. He and Hope had opened the Ozark Stampede, aka the Western Fun Rodeo, featuring bull riding, bareback bronco riding, calf roping, and steer wrestling.

Hope kept things going while Tex was "away" with all-girl

rodeos that included bullwhip demonstrations where the whip-pers cut a newspaper down to postage stamp–sized pieces; guest appearances by the likes of country star Porter Wagoner; and dog shows with a dozen or more at a time doing tricks. Posters also promised bear wrestling and mule diving but I never witnessed those. I still consider that a gaping void in my life, along with seeing the head-on locomotive wrecks they used to have at state fairs.

"How's it going, Mrs. Varner?" I'd ask when Hope walked in the front door.

"Same ol' same ol'," she'd reply.

Hope Varner was later inducted into the Cowgirl Hall of Fame. I had a crush on her. But I was born too late. I'm sorry now I never asked for an autographed picture.

* * *

Larry Albright said some of his greatest ideas, indeed one of the greatest concepts in tourist attractions since the Hanging Gardens of Babylon, never reached fruition.

He had his eye on an old wooden tourist boat, which he would rename the *Oz-Ark* and conduct fanciful tours unlike any before. He had in mind cutting a large hole in the center and covering it with Plexiglas.

He looked up, closed his eyes, and began reciting the spiel he would have delivered to a packed boat at five bucks a head: "We are now passing over the lost city of Linn Creek, submersed in almost *biblical* fashion by the coming of these waters...Glimpses of this modern-day Atlantis can be captured through Aqua-Scope, the space-age window installed in the hull of this vessel."

He paused to gauge my reaction. I was spellbound. "Unfortunately," he continued, "these fathoms are sometimes murky and Linn Creek cannot be seen. But postcards with drawings of the submerged buildings are available in our Neptune's Corral gift shop as you debark." The postcards would be free with the purchase of a box of Ozark pralines.

He paused again before reciting the denouement, one that would have had all of central Missouri talking.

"As we enter the next cove, keep your eyes peeled," he said, "for that rarest of all breeds...the freshwater Ozark seal!"

With that, Larry broke from his script, then let forth a long, loud belly laugh.

"You've never seen an Ozark seal?" he asked.

"No," I answered. "What do they look like?"

"It would have looked a lot like a kid like you swimming around with a brown hood over his face," he said, "for a dollar an hour."

Chapter Four

Uncle Ed

$\mathcal{U}$ncle Ed was in charge. No doubt about it. He was a colonel in World War II and never quite stopped being one. When he walked into a room you half expected everyone to snap to attention and salute. And so, I suspect, did he. He didn't speak so much as he barked.

He served in the Signal Corps as head of the army pictorial service in Europe. You've probably seen his work. It carried the History Channel for years and years. He had a library of film canisters full of priceless footage in his basement

Famous Hollywood directors like Frank Capra, John Huston, and John Ford were actually under his command—at least on the organizational chart—making documentary, propaganda, and training films that were far more artistic than they needed to be: Capra's *Why We Fight*; Huston's *The Battle of San Pietro*; and Ford's less heralded *Sex Hygiene*.

"Really, Uncle Ed? You could give orders to Hollywood big shots? Oscar winners?"

"Hellll yes," he answered in a low-key, understated way he saved for dismissing obvious questions.

One of my basement favorites was a reel of outtakes of Ronald Reagan giving a class to soldiers on some boring, pedestrian topic or other—the kind that put soldiers to sleep, causing them to fall out of the bleachers. Each time Ronnie tried to pull down a movie screen over a blackboard, the screen snapped back up and spun like a propeller. As gentlemanly as Reagan was said to be, on his third attempt he appeared to be saying "Son-of-a-bitch!" the flapping screen drowning out the audio. "Great guy..." Ed commented. Reagan had been to the lake, gone out on Ed's boat, the *Arrowhead*, and signed the logbook. "...for a Republican," Ed added.

Uncle Ed's war was longer than most. He had hotel suites in London and Paris, "stocked with scotch and Red Cross girls."

There are photos—not really incriminating, but they do show Red Cross girls and soldiers in dress uniforms drinking from highball glasses. Doubt you'll ever see Uncle Ed's war photos in a Ken Burns documentary.

The story goes that he didn't return stateside to his wife, Aunt Janet (my father's younger sister), and his two stepsons, Art and Charlie (one from each of her previous marriages), until a year after VE Day.

His war stories were different from most too. For example: "We were in a café in a small town in France drinking French 75s [gin, sugar, lemon, champagne]. The Germans were closing in. When the bartender stopped shaking the cocktail shaker we could hear their tanks rumbling toward the edge of town. As we ran for the door, I brushed by a girl on a barstool, who turned to me and said, 'Kiss me, I'm comin'.' So I did. And I'm pretty sure she did too." Big laughs.

The thing was, he first told me this one when I was fourteen or fifteen and I had no idea what he was talking about. Did "comin'" mean she was leaving with them, or what?

"Those were different times," he mused, reflecting on the psycho-sexual effects of the war on the local citizenry, one of the few experts on this particular subject I've encountered.

"In London and Paris the girls would go to bed with guys— hell, they'd suggest it!—because they weren't sure they'd be alive the next day.

"We weren't either. In the Pigalle, the professional girls would tell us, 'It's only money, honey, and you can't take it with you.'"

On his triumphant, belated return stateside he led a convoy of trucks carrying French champagne and other spoils of war down Fifth Avenue in New York to the posh Pierre Hotel, where he set up a command post before eventually returning home to Illinois.

His father, Pappy, owned the *Dairyman's Journal* and a small resort hotel at Lake of the Ozarks, wherever the hell that was. I recall being at his home in East St. Louis when he told of the resort going to hell—bottle caps and cigarette butts around the pool—and in need of someone to run the place right.

I don't know what convinced Ed and Janet to go down there "amongst the brush apes," as she jokingly referred to the local folks. Maybe it wasn't such a bad alternative to traveling from farm to farm, small town to small town, selling ad space to teet squeezers.

* * *

Ed made a big splash in the small pond, living the life of a wealthy big shot while he was actually the owner-manager of a modest forty-one-room hotel in the Ozarks. Only a man like Ed could pull it off. And did he ever.

He drove Cadillacs, two a year, a new convertible in summer, which he traded in for a new hardtop each fall, "when the ashtrays got full." No one knew exactly what the deal was, but Billy Pearl, the Caddy dealer in Mexico, Missouri, came to the lodge a lot, staying in one of the best rooms, perhaps at a favorable rate.

Ed bragged about writing off his clothing expenses on his tax returns, not to mention his thirty-four-foot cabin cruiser, on which he entertained "clients." (And who among us is not a potential client of a hotel?) His yacht was not all that big by today's standards, but bigger than most on the lake back then—and that's what mattered.

His payroll was seasonal, and possibly in violation of minimum wage laws. He hired college students each summer and paid them a pittance. In the lengthy off season, Ed and Janet traveled widely and extravagantly "around the world," writing off their trips to Arrowhead's 'Round the World Gift Shop, a ten-by-fifteen-foot shop on the front porch, possibly named by his tax consultant.

Customers paid cash for rooms and meals; we didn't really have credit cards yet. Leastwise, not down in those parts.

Ed made a practice of taking a wad of the larger bills from the cash register and stuffing it into his front pants pocket (apart from the other proceeds, which were in a deposit pouch) before driving down to make his regular bank deposit. He often asked me to tag along.

I remember thinking on those blissful rides that this must be what it's like getting from place to place in heaven, sitting in the overstuffed red leather passenger seat of Uncle Ed's big white boat of a car, a Caddy convertible, cruising smoothly and quietly on fat whitewall tires, the gently passing breeze barely detectable on those warm, sunny summer mornings.

Ed wore sunglasses—back when only movie stars and Ed wore sunglasses—and silk floral shirts—way, way back before Jimmy Buffett. He wore Bermuda shorts and expensive leather sandals purchased in London. No other male in the Ozarks wore sandals. Well, one.

Two fingers of his left hand rested lightly on the bottom of the steering wheel. Two fingers of his right cradled a cigar, as naturally as if he'd been born with it there.

His hair was slicked straight back, reddish, like his thin mustache. The backs of his hands bore a few flaky red spots from too much sun, as mine do now, fifty years down the road. Back then there was no such thing as too much sun, even for us redheads.

(We didn't have SPF. Sun was good! Essential to life. Ancient cultures worshipped the sun. Who are these ingrates who would *block the sun*? One day, *too much* sunblock may be blamed for skin disease. But I digress.)

A weighted cup holder straddled the center hump, holding an insulated plastic highball glass, filled—at 11:30 a.m.—with three fingers of Ballantine's scotch and water.

The top was down and the factory air conditioner on low, because Pierre, Ed's miniature black poodle, liked it that way (Pierre dined on prime rib au jus for dinner). He had his rear paws on the back seat and his front paws on the center console. His ears were flapping gently in the artificial breeze. He seemed to be smiling.

He went everywhere with Ed: in the car, on his cruiser, even perched, almost impossibly, on the slick, varnished bow of his speedboat.

Once, when Ed was frantically trying to figure out who had driven off with his car from a party, someone suggested: "Maybe Pierre took it." To which Ed replied: "No, he's right here with me."

Ed turned into the unpaved parking lot at Bank of Lake of the Ozarks, kicking up dust. He flicked a switch beneath the steering wheel that triggered the sound of a cow loudly "mooing" (not standard equipment) under the hood.

Colonel G. Edwin Popkess ("Popkess," an English name) had arrived.

He grabbed his money pouch and pushed open the hefty, vault-like Caddy door, whipped off his sunglasses, took the cigar from his mouth, and it was showtime! We burst into the bank with all the subtlety of Bonnie and Clyde.

"Hello, Jimmy!" he bellowed at the bank president.

"Morning, Colonel!" Jim shot back.

There was a line at the teller's window. For the other people. Ed handed the bank president his deposit pouch.

"You bein' a good boy?" Ed boomed.

"Tryin'," Jim said.

"We had a helluva weekend," Ed said. "Full up and two hundred and fifty people in the dining room Saturday night. Gonna be a helluva summer."

"Hope so," Jim said, a bit sheepishly.

"Hope so!?" Ed shot back "Hell, it gets bigger and better every summer. No hopin' about it."

Jimmy counted out what money was in the pouch, and handed Ed a receipt.

"Take care, old buddy!" Ed blared.

"Hello, beautiful!" he shouted at a plain, middle-aged, chunky female teller.

"Mornin', Mr. Popkess," was all the teller could muster. That and a full blush.

"Hello, Johnny Boy," Ed said, greeting Johnny Boy from the Sunoco station. Ed never forgot a name or a face. And treated everyone, from the bank president to a gas station attendant, the same. That's something I picked up from him.

In parting, Ed shouted to one and all: "You all stay out of trouble now!" And exited stage right.

Other customers looked at us and each other, wondering just who in the hell were these guys anyhow?

Darting out like we'd robbed the place, I headed to the car, shaking my head in disbelief as I often did after playing a bit part in one of Ed's performances. I looked back and saw the extras staring out the window. The big Caddy kicked gravel back at the bank before blasting off up the highway.

I really didn't belong in that car. I don't know who did, somebody probably, but it wasn't me.

* * *

In a word, Ed had it "dicked," as folks in these parts called that blissful state of serenity and well-being that comes with having it all—and knowing it.

A lot of guys working at the lodge wanted to grow up to have it dicked just like him. One managed to do it. Jim Chappell opened a highly successful sports bar in Kansas City, Chappell's Restaurant and Sports Museum, where he was the boss, entertained people, and traveled the world. Just like Ed, who told Jim to call when he was a millionaire. He did.

Others tried their own misguided ways to be like Ed, such as taking hotel management courses, where they teach things like saying "my pleasure" no matter what the request.

Maybe you're calling the front desk to tell them that your toilet's overflowing and horrible wastewater is flooding your entire room and they must fix it immediately and the clerk says sweetly: "My pleasure, Mr. Geist." They can't teach you to be Uncle Ed.

Ed and Janet lived in a handsome stone and dark wood lakefront home with a spacious screened porch that jutted out into the high branches of tall, leafy trees. A four-seat rail tram transported passengers some sixty feet down to his covered dock. Seems ridiculous until you need to go *up* the hill after a day of cocktails aboard the *Arrowhead*.

On a typical workday (*half* a normal person's workday; dicked) Ed awoke in the morning and called the hotel—my cue to deliver his pot of coffee and newspapers. (I'll take a wild guess and say he was probably the only *Wall Street Journal* subscriber at Lake of the Ozarks.)

He wanted his morning delivery pronto so I drove the lodge station wagon as fast and recklessly as possible down the narrow curvy road, the coffeepot wedged tightly between my ankles to keep it upright against the g-forces on the curves. Some mornings the g-forces won and my feet were bathed in scalding coffee. "Aieeee!" I'd scream and do a one-eighty for a refill.

Opening his porch door set an attached bell jingling, announcing visitors. And there he was, sitting at the kitchen table looking almost Hefnerian in a purple silk bathrobe. He was a little gruff in the mornings as you might expect of someone who drank as much scotch as he did, and was especially cranky on paydays.

The kitchen was always spick-and-span. Janet never cooked. Ever. "Take a look for yourself," she laughed, "the tags are still on the pots and pans." She and Ed ate every meal out, usually at the hotel.

He'd drink the entire pot of coffee and start to twitch a little. Twitching was not good. It was a warning sign that he was agitated and not to be messed with. Back away slowly. Scotch would later take the edge off.

His commute to work was about three minutes (dicked). He had no one to answer to so he could report when he damned well pleased (dicked), although his military mind-set had him arriving within five or ten minutes of zero-eight-hundred hours most every day.

His eagle eye never missed a blemish. He'd barge through

the front door and bark: "Billy! There's a cigarette butt under a rocking chair on the porch. And a beer bottle in the bushes. This isn't some damned honky-tonk!"

"Chappell!" he'd yell at Jim. "There are three big, ugly cardboard boxes outside the front door! Looks like a shipping depot. Put 'em out back! Do I have to do all the thinking around here?!"

"Good morning, Puggy," he'd say to the desk clerk. "Everything copacetic?"

"Fine and dandy, Mr. Popkess," she'd reply, always accentuating the positive, which seemed to work,

Ed was very efficient. He would inspect, noting things that needed attention and dressing down those who weren't doing their jobs. Then he was off, heading back down to the house, mixing himself a drink and backing the *Arrowhead* out of the dock on a lunch, and, need I add "booze,"cruise, with a few guests aboard.

From many a cruise with Cap'n Ed, it was my understanding of Missouri maritime law that each vessel was to carry one life jacket and a fifth of liquor for every person aboard.

Hey, this wasn't ocean boating, where you had to pay attention. Lakes make sense. Shallow by the shore. Deep in the middle. No rocks or sandbars lurking just below the surface to knock holes in the hull and shear off propellers. No tides to monitor, No depth gauges or ship-to-shore radios. No red-right-return. None of that.

Vigilance? Sobriety? Not all that necessary back then.

He'd return about three for his afternoon nap, which I always thought was alcohol related but have since discovered is also a symptom of age. I work at home a lot and have noticed that my twenty-minute naps have ballooned to sixty. Ed's were about an hour. He'd rise, pour himself a drink as naturally as putting on his pants, and head back to the lodge, where he served as official greeter for the dining room.

He was a born politician. He seemed to remember the name of almost anyone he'd ever met. He'd ask where they were from, and no matter how small a town would say he knew it well, and would prove it by asking about a person, place, or thing. Amazing. Think it came from traveling the boondocks for the *Dairyman's Journal.*

* * *

Every morning when he arrived at the lodge Uncle Ed would take his seat at the front table for yet more coffee and two poached eggs. He snagged every employee who came past to interrogate them about the social events of the previous evening, about who was with whom, and just how "with" them they were. Piecing together this ever-changing social puzzle was his hobby. He enjoyed astounding all of us with all he knew.

This day, Jim Chappell was the first to be questioned.

"Party at the pool last night?" Ed asked.

"Yessir," Jim answered.

"You with Gina?"

"Yessir."

"Gettin' any of that?' Ed probed.

Jim laughed and said, "Do I have to answer that?"

Ed was a matchmaker, and a good one, with the record to prove it. Short term and long. Countless summer romances and several marriages. There's something to be said for matchmaking, whether by parents or dating services. Arranged marriages enjoy a high success rate worldwide, but then so do drive-through Vegas marriages with an "Elvis" presiding. So they say.

One of Ed's great matches was Gina, a willowy waitress, and Jim, who met at Arrowhead one summer when she was a lowly housekeeper and he was an even lowlier weed cutter.

Gina and Jim were married just down the hill at Our Lady of the Lake Church. Ed went all out on this one. If Jim was driving up to the lodge from Drury University in southwest Missouri to work a fall weekend, Ed would fly his plane up to Northeast Missouri State to pick up Gina.

Ed wasn't just a hopeless romantic. He desperately needed help on busy fall weekends. He sometimes flew to Bolivar, Missouri, to pick up another waitress, Marilyn, at Southwest Baptist University, then on to Drury University in Springfield to pick up Jim (on weekends Jim wasn't driving a hundred miles to the lake), and yet another waitress, Karen.

Like all things, flying with Uncle Ed was a little different. He piloted a small Cessna and allowed smoking. Back then all planes did. Hard to imagine now, sitting shoulder to shoulder with passengers puffing away.

When I flew with Ed, he'd light up a cigar and, intent on his flying, he'd unconsciously flick the ashes onto my lap. I'd only bring this to his attention when my pants began to smolder.

Gina and Jim's marriage has lasted more than fifty years. Photos show that Wheezer, a friend from Champaign, and I were in the wedding party, although neither of us remember much about it, probably owing to the prolonged open bar reception Ed held in the Pow Wow Room after the ceremony.

Gina and Jim's wedding. Ed is next to Jim, Wheezer is on the far right, and I'm next to Wheezer.

He gave the newly betrothed couple a credit card to pay for their honeymoon and sent them on their way toward Kansas City.

But they continued westward all the way to the Broadmoor, the five-star resort hotel in Colorado Springs—making Ed's wedding gift more extravagant than he'd perhaps intended.

Ed put together even the most unlikely matches. Sharon, a cute waitress with a sunny disposition, and Slugger, an often hot-tempered bellhop, a nephew on Ed's side of the family, who was fired every couple of weeks. But Ed always took him back. Sharon and Slugger have also celebrated their golden wedding anniversary.

He was also responsible for joining in holy matrimony Jim Murphy, the tall, ultra-thin cook who was our straw boss, and Sandy Sinclair, a blond waitress, the daughter of Boofie, a genial cook from Lawrence, Kansas. Jim worked at the lodge year-round, taking the lodge station wagon to classes at Lincoln University in Jefferson City.

He served as a helicopter pilot in Vietnam. He returned unharmed to the States only to commit suicide. I asked Ed why he thought Jim had done that and he snapped angrily: "How the hell should I know?! Maybe he just didn't want to live anymore!"

Ed was not keen on reflection, particularly on such an unpleasant subject.

As you might imagine, with Ed doing the hiring, the waitress corps was an attractive lot, with Betty Selby oft mentioned as the fairest of them all. She acknowledged she once received a hundred-dollar tip. (The other waitresses said it was more than once.) She babysat for guests and played bridge with them.

One couple who gave her a hundred-dollar tip told her to buy a dress for her first day on her new job. She wore that new dress to teach her third-grade class in Oak Park, Illinois.

Betty had to ward off the unwelcome advances, to include suggestive comments and occasional touches, of male customers, often businessmen in small groups acting as though they hadn't been away from home in a long, long time and were, in addition, three sheets to the wind.

"We didn't complain," Betty recalled, "we liked our jobs and needed the money." That was then.

She had a plan. On a shopping trip to Eldon, she bought a "diamond" engagement ring at the five-and-dime. She put it in a handy spot in the kitchen and when necessary slipped it on her finger to show to aggressive male diners. She'd tell them that she was the fiancée of that big guy behind the front desk (Ralph), who she'd clued in to cross his arms and give them a stern stare. All the waitresses used the ring at one time or another.

As fate would have it, Betty did marry Ralph, who became a doctor.

Van was a middle-aged waitress and self-described gold-digger. She married an aging, well-to-do dining room regular from Mexico, Missouri: J. B. Arthur, described in his obituary as a "brick magnate." Not quite gold, but many, many bricks.

Another waitress, Karen, married into Lake of the Ozarks royalty. Karen had a sparkle in her eyes, was quick to laugh, and up for anything. Some nights a group would head out to a Mexican restaurant across the dam, El Sarape, where one evening she chugged a small container of habanero sauce on a ten-dollar bet. She couldn't speak for nearly a week. Severe esophageal inflammation.

She married Larry Fry, who was a dining room regular. His father was the postmaster, who was usually stripped to his T-shirt on hot days behind the counter. An unassuming look for a man who owned vast swaths of property on the strip. His son, Larry, who was in fact *the* Larry of the fabled *Larry Don* cruise boat, passed away some years ago, after which the *Larry Don* sank.

Quite a record Ed had, and he wasn't about to rest on his laurels.

Ed's waitress this morning, a fetching young woman, came over to ask if he'd like more coffee.

"Yes, darling," he said to her. "Let me take a look at you," he said, gently grasping her free hand while looking her up and down.

"You have big beautiful eyes," he said. Check. He was right about that.

She blushed. "Thank you, Mr. Popkess."

"What a great smile," he added. Check.

"And...look at that body."

Awww, Ed! Did you have to *say* it? He did. He was Ed.

Sorry! I should have warned you about Uncle Ed. He could be rather crude at times—a lot of times. Maybe most. Those of us who knew the man were always braced for him to say something of the sort, something untoward. We cringed as we always did when we sensed one of those gems coming.

"Have you met the great Billy Geist?" Ed asked, with me standing right there.

"Yes," she said.

"What do you think?"

"Seems nice. We don't know each other very well yet."

(I liked the "yet.")

"Why don't you get to know each other better," Ed suggested. "Break away and head up to the Oaks tonight." The Oaks was a beer joint just up the road, frequented by Arrowhead employees.

"Would you like that?" he asked her.

"Sounds like fun," she answered. (I could not speak.) "You two might wind up having a summer romance," he said, brazenly, totally jumping the gun. I don't know if she blushed but I did.

Notably, at least to me, she said nothing to deflate or refute his "summer romance" comment. As for me, I was thinking it was one helluva good idea.

I was excited about our date at the Oaks. I think she was too. We smiled whenever we spotted each other that day. She did indeed have a great smile and big brown eyes and that other thing.

Her name was Dana. She was eighteen, had grown up on a farm not far from here, just graduated high school, and was heading off this fall to nursing school in Springfield. I was two years older, but still too young to buy beer. However, I'd had the foresight to hold a premature twenty-first birthday party at the Oaks, complete with a cake, candles, and a group counting down to midnight when I would, ostensibly if not actually, come of age. That was all the proof the bartender needed.

Dana and I sat in a booth, which was good, more intimate, provided I had anything to say, which was not much at first, but more and more as the level of Falstaff in the pitcher dropped precipitously. The beer seemed to me to be making my conversation not only more plentiful but more fascinating, as well. She even laughed a few times.

We got a little tipsy. We played the shuffle puck bowling machine. As I pushed the silver metal puck down the two-foot alley she grasped my arm tightly as if she had money riding on the game. She cheered strikes. When it was her turn I stood closely behind her. So closely it seemed my denim pants and her polyester shorts might synthesize into some new miracle fabric. This seemed to be fine with her.

This was good. She was most attractive. I hoped this wasn't going to be a problem. I mean she could have been way less attractive and still have been plenty attractive enough for me. Know what I mean?

I was scared to death of girls, especialy attractive ones. Had been for years, since I was scorched by the all-too-atractive girl next door. But this could be a whole new beginning, thanks to Uncle Ed, the matchmaker. It would have taken weeks or months for me to summon the courage to ask Dana to go with me to the Oaks. It took a bold, offensive, crude force to get the ball rolling. Uncle Ed. Matchmaking isn't always pretty.

After dropping Dana off at the She Shack, where the waitresses lived, I went home to bed, but was unable to sleep, thinking about our fresh, budding relationship in that special libidinous way that sort of ruins everything.

Chapter Five

The Chili Pond

*N*ow I don't want to say that working at a resort the first summer wasn't all I dreamed it would be, but: Where were the girls in bikinis? When do we go water-skiing? Why hasn't the nepotism kicked in?

Such dark thoughts filled my head as I sloshed in high, black rubber boots through fetid waters collecting on the surface of the lodge's open-air septic system, twelve red tile sewer pipes emptying into a forty-by-forty-foot sandbox known as the Chili Pond.

The theory of sanitation engineering and sciences behind this system was that noxious fluids would flow down from the headwaters, or commodes, seep in and flow through the sand until the saturation point was reached and the contaminated waters could seep no more. The theory posited that somehow in all this flowing and seeping the water would somehow be purified. You take the first sip.

The discharge, about the shade of stout English breakfast tea, would begin collecting on the surface and the warm summer sunshine would bring out the rich, full-bodied aroma.

Who you gonna call? The Septic Solutions Squad. Us: Two of the lowliest on the organizational chart, two with the least time of service, were issued rubber boots and armed with shovels to churn the sands, for what our straw boss, Jim Murphy, called "a day at the beach." Funny guy, that Jim. It was always two guys—the buddy system—in case one was overcome.

"Look!" shouted John, my partner, hoisting something that looked like a six-inch translucent version of a boot dangling on the end of his shovel. A gift from the sea.

"Hold it up to your ear," I replied, "and you can hear the sound of flushing."

Today, the Chili Pond would probably be declared a Superfund site, crawling with EPA crews in haz mat suits. (Disregard this remark if we don't have an EPA anymore.)

Just as Jim called this "a day at the beach," so too did he refer to swinging a long-handled weed cutter back and forth for hours on the back hill "practicing your golf swing." That Jim. He had a million of 'em.

John was a friend from home, who joined me at the lodge my first summer, envisioning the same bikinis and ski boats I did. His mom came several weeks early to pick him up after too much sun 'n' fun in the Chili Pond, weed wacking,

and spending most of his meager salary on jumbo bottles of calamine lotion.

He let out a yell one morning as we were cutting on the back hill when he came upon a big black snake. I couldn't stand snakes and lived in fear every time we cut weeds from then on. We didn't really have snakes in Champaign, just the very rare short, skinny green "garden snake" not much bigger than a worm. Even today I prefer an urban environment where all the world's concrete and you can see what lies ahead even if it's a mugger.

(Here's how I feel about snakes: In Vietnam, when our base camp was under nightly rocket attacks, everyone slept in a sandbagged bunker except me. I'd seen a snake slithering out of the bunker and never went back. I knew then that I would rather die than see a snake.)

There were also special projects, such as diving into the lake to force empty fifty-five-gallon drums under Ed's dock for added flotation. The barrels had been previously filled with gelatinous creosote, a toxic substance now banned in many states. Pete and I were covered with the stuff. When purple and red patches broke out all over our bodies, Jim thoughtfully washed us down with gasoline.

In the afternoons, we'd collect dirty laundry from the linen closets, wrap it in bundles twice our size then stagger under their enormous weight to the pickup bins on the She Shack porch.

Chapter Six

Extreme Dishwashing

*S*ometimes our workdays were extended to include night dishwashing. What was this? The Decathlon of Degradation?

Arrowhead's dishwasher was not something manufactured by Maytag's industrial division. It was us. Two-man crews.

Waitresses crashed through the swinging kitchen doors, precariously balancing metal trays heaping with filthy, greasy, scummy—and quite heavy—Frankoma dishes, then heave them into the rack. Wheezer (an asthmatic given this nickname by junior high classmates, a group not known for their sensitivity) would scrape the scraps into a barrel, then throw the dishes into a large tub of scalding, soapy water. He'd wash them, then gently lower them (if business was slow) into the rinse tub, or toss them (if it was busy).

Glasses went into a third tub filled with cold water (to make them sparkle) and all of it went helter-skelter onto a towel-covered counter to dry.

On, say, a Saturday night in August, you had to be ready for Extreme Dishwashing. Psyched. With a warrior mentality. One night Wheezer and I bound our heads in dish towels in what I would call a vaguely Arabian-ninja (or possibly two-guys-suffering-from-extreme-head-wounds) look. I took to calling him "Larry," because "Lawrence" seemed overly formal. He called me "Saudi."

The dishes came in at a fast pace, but we handled them, no problem. The pace accelerated but we were still fine. A couple of bad-ass dishwashers, I tell ya. Then suddenly we were hit with a tsunami of dirty dishes that came flooding through that damnable, heartless swinging kitchen door.

Code Red! We were losing ground! Suddenly the Wheez and I looked like Lucy and Ethel on the assembly line at that chocolate factory. Within a minute, the rack was completely filled with trays, stacked, precariously, atop one another when Sharon, a petite waitress, staggered in with a big tray of about her own weight. There was simply nowhere to put it.

Chef Glen took notice, calling out to Wheez and me: "What the hell are you two doing over there, playing with each other?"—a remark audible to those at the closest tables in the dining room.

Glen would be Glen Clymore, Arrowhead's longtime chef, who packed up every fall when the season at the lake was over, and headed out to California—Van Nuys, was it?—where he worked as a chef all winter until his return here every spring.

"Shut up, fry cook!" I shot back (not a snappy retort but the only thing I could come up with on the spur of the moment to insult a chef), causing Chef Glen to retort something about coming over there to kick my bony ass, and as a former boxer, he undoubtedly could have…except…I was thinking…he was a good thirty years older than me and almost certainly drunk. You could say Glen had an alcohol-based lifestyle, except we didn't have lifestyles back then. He liked to drink morning, afternoon, and night.

I took Sharon's tray and set it—where? There was nowhere. I set it atop the garbage barrel.

I suddenly noticed something both alarming and deeply distressing. Wheezer's hot dishwater, now cool, looked like a vat of chicken noodle soup, cloudy with chunks of food floating in it.

We had to drain the huge tubs and refill them, which would take a good six to eight minutes, time enough for us to be buried alive in dirty dishes.

We were defenseless. The onslaught of the big trays continued. I slid the next one under the washtubs. Then another and another, until I had to kick the dishes to make them stay put under there. Probably half of Arrowhead's tableware was under the tubs and taking heavy casualties.

I was later told it could have been even worse. Marilyn, a waitress, recalled a busy night when the dishwashers didn't show up at all: "Dirty dishes were piled on every flat surface," she said. Ethyl Pearl, who was a guest almost every summer weekend, went back in the kitchen to help.

Wheezer was laughing uncontrollably, but then, he would. A

lesser man might have cracked. Indeed, on just such a frantic moment on another busy night, Terry, a teenager from Webster Groves, Missouri, flipped out and began throwing dirty dishes into the trash barrel and smashing them with the end of a broom handle. It was like hand-to-hand trench warfare in World War I.

"We kept running out of silverware," Marilyn recalled, "until we discovered that the newly assigned dishwashers didn't want to be bothered with it and were sticking it in the old coffee grounds and throwing it down the hill behind the kitchen."

There was always a good deal of plate and dish pilfering. Many dishes were shaped like arrowheads and women would furtively stick them in their purses or even down the fronts of their dresses.

At long last, on our fateful evening, the restaurant finally closed, but for Wheez and me, our Arabian night at the washtubs had only begun. The much-hated, unwieldy, stubbornly filthy pots and pans awaited.

Chapter Seven

Another Day, Another Dollar

*W*e couldn't complain. We were at the top of Ed's pay scale: five dollars a day.

For bellhops and waitresses (who made tips) it was one dollar. A buck. A dollar a day. You've heard the old expression "Another day, another dollar." At Arrowhead it was more than an expression.

"Hell, the bellhops at the Chase Park Plaza in St. Louis have to *buy* their jobs," Ed reminded us, time and again.

By now you must be asking yourselves: Why?! Why would anyone want to work so long and so hard for so little? With smiles on their faces?

I've done a couple of TV pieces on ice fishing. Viewers see thousands of shivering men on a windswept frozen lake in Minnesota drilling holes in the thick ice and dangling lines down in hopes of catching a perch or a walleye and viewers ask: Why? Because men will do anything—anything!—

to get away from their families and drink beer. Ice fishing proves it.

Well, it turns out young men and women will too. A summer at Arrowhead offered an opportunity to be on our own and away from incessant interrogation from parents about where we were last night, with whom, what time we got home, were we drinking beer, and on and on.

And, there is the distinct possibility that our parents didn't really mind seeing us go.

Most, perhaps all, of us were from middle-class families and trying to pay our way through college. Waitresses could clear from $1,000 to $1,500 for the summer, bellhops $800 or so. Now this may not seem like a lot, but at the University of Illinois in the sixties my tuition for a semester was—parents, do not commit hara-kiri—$135.

We learned to work hard at Arrowhead. But we were free, unsophisticated, and easily amused (sounds like the title of a Clint Eastwood–Mel Brooks production), drinking lots of beer, laughing uproariously, dancing like wild banshees in the Pow Wow Room, pushing fully clothed, cavorting colleagues into the pool, heading down to Ron's Town House (one account claims eight or nine passengers riding there in and on Bebe's VW), a dance hall below the dam, having late-night repasts at Evelyn's Rathskeller or "Sharpies" (El Sarape)...

Now, to give Ed his due, it was $5 or $1 *plus* room and board.

Board was anything we wanted for breakfast and lunch.

Dinner was that day's special. There were ways to supplement your diet. Annie's extraordinary deep-dish apple pie with vanilla sauce was the most pilfered item in the kitchen.

"I tasted my first lobster ever," said Ellen, who worked in the kitchen and grabbed the crustaceans off trays of dirty dishes. How could anyone pay these prices for lobsters and then not eat them?

Sadie, a head-turning beauty from Sedalia, had her mouth stuffed with hush puppies every time I glanced her way, which was quite often. She gained an estimated fifteen pounds on her summer hush puppy diet. It wasn't always pretty, watching her wildly snatching the deep-fried dough balls as they rolled off trays toward the garbage.

I would sometimes drop by the kitchen quite late when Glen was already in, preparing for the next day. We'd chat and sometimes out of the blue he'd ask if I was hungry—and who isn't after a long night of carousing, with dinner but a distant memory eight hours before?

Glen broiled a twelve-ounce steak, fried up some American Lyonnaise potatoes, and served me at a rusty old desk hidden from view way back in the rear of the kitchen. Despite the ambiance, those remain some of the best meals I've ever had. I made a habit of strolling through the kitchen late at night to say hello to Glen.

For lunch and dinner, the grungier among us (outdoor workers) dined at a small banquet table on the She Shack screened porch next to mountains of dirty laundry. There was lively, if less than sharp-witted, banter. We seemed to always find ways to amuse ourselves.

It was at this table where Wheezer and I created an act that would later (about fifty years later) be called the Aqua-Tones.

We'd belt out the opening line from "Ebb Tide": "First the tide rushes in..."

Whereupon I'd pour—with gusto—the contents of a full water pitcher into Wheezer's empty pitcher, from a good height to produce a hearty splashing sound as befits the tide rushing in.

Then, the next line, "Plants a kiss on the shore," and I'd slop a dainty amount, a kiss, into Wheezer's pitcher.

"Then rolls out to sea...and the sea is very still once more..." Heavy pour with abrupt stop.

"So I rush to your side..."

Wheezer pours with gusto.

"Like the oncoming tide..."

And so on, with increasingly sloppy pouring that ends with the finale: two of us pouring water on each other's heads.

It never really attracted a wide audience.

Mealtimes, some including the Aqua-Tones dinner theater, were quite a departure from those back home.

* * *

That was the "board" part. As for "room," the guys did their rooming on the lower level of Janet and Ed's lakefront home, which upon entry was just a darkened basement with a toilet and an industrial-sized gray concrete washbasin for shaving and brushing teeth, and splashing on English Leather after-shave that we hoped would sway reluctant females. But the view brightened dramatically in the next three rooms, which had large windows looking out on the lawn and the lake.

The rooms were filled with single beds, two in a dark, dank space beneath the garage next to a dark, dank shower where molds of the world were on exhibit. These beds were the last to be claimed.

Next to last were two twins by the ironing board and washer-dryer. Although it must be said that a dryer can have a beneficial lulling effect on those falling asleep or passing out for the evening. Bellhops wore white shirts, which we ironed ourselves and it showed.

This whetted my appetite for a CBS piece on the increasingly (but still not very) popular sport of "extreme ironing" in England. I competed, ironing a shirt at the main gate of Windsor Castle as the palace guard looked on. They aren't supposed to crack smiles but one did before bobbies ran me off. On that trip, I went for high tea at the five-star Brown's Hotel where Ed served in World War II.

Next, downstairs at Ed's lake house, was a small and rather attractive room with its stone wall and the advantage of having just one bed (no roomies). This one went to the first male summer employee to arrive, at least until the one with the most seniority threw him out. The attractive private room did have the unattractive tendency to attract the occasional scorpion.

The last room was a large, bright one with wall-to-wall-windows on two sides and five, six, or seven single beds lining the edges. They surrounded Janet's art studio, where she painted rather ghastly works—you really had to see the clown portrait—that, when hung on the walls of the lodge with little portrait lights illuminating them museum style, somehow sold! I hadn't yet learned that out there in the "serious" art world, preschool, refrigerator-door-quality paintings were sold to wealthy collectors for millions.

The screened windows were open to catch the breeze. My screen was something of a work of art itself. Someone, probably me, regurgitated out the window one evening without realizing that the screen was there. When the screen was wiped clean: voilà! An impression that bore an uncanny likeness to Richard M. Nixon.

Ed had a double dock for his twenty-two-or-so-foot Chris-Craft speedboat and his thirty-four-foot cabin cruiser. A houseboat was also docked alongside, that spot bestowed by Ed to Arrowhead's best customer, Bill Justus, a doctor from Pleasanton, Kansas, who drove down to the lodge in his Corvette every Friday night for at least thirty-five years beginning in about 1955. In that golden age of playboys, Doc Justus was hall of fame caliber. He arrived and left alone. As Uncle Ed oft said: "Bringing a girl down here would be like taking a ham sandwich to a banquet."

Doc would ply the waters with music blasting, telling all the world the party was here! He'd have four or five beauties in

77

colorful bikinis festooning the roof of his houseboat. How did he do it? The same scene every weekend. I went down once to cast them off and to see if the girls in bikinis just might be decorative blow-up dolls.

Doc was not tall, dark, or strikingly handsome and walked with a slight limp. But he was cool, laid-back, fun, confident of the outcome. I lusted after some of these girls, but I looked and leered with no clue how to get to where I wanted to be. I needed and wanted everything to happen naturally and immediately. I figured, and quite rightly, I believe, that these tanned, sculpted goddesses might not be all that interested in a scrawny six-foot 155-pound kid with skin that was somewhere between ceiling white and translucent. I was considered funny, but these beauties dancing on the roof of Doc's houseboat didn't give a damn about that. They wanted beefcake. For me, summer was always the cruelest season. Days were worse than nights. I wore long pants rather than shorts even on the hottest days, to hide my skinny, pasty legs. I tried tanning cream one summer, but it proved closer to Sherwin-Williams than St. Tropez Whipped Self-Tanning Mousse and it collected at my elbows and knees, turning them a contrasting burnt umber hue. Plus I forgot to apply any to my face.

Across the cove was Arrowhead Yacht Club, where some thirty or more cabin cruisers with catchy names like *Boozin' and Cruisin'* and *Wet Dream* docked. At night we could lie there in the dark, listening to the boats taxi slowly in and out of the cove. I especially liked the powerful low rumbling and gurgling the speedboats made as their exhaust pipes dipped in and out of the water. Once past the breakwater, which was a giant fallen tree lashed in place at the cove's entrance, they'd hit the throttle and disappear with a roar into the night.

You could hear revelers on boats coming a mile away. One night I waited on the dock for a boatload I was to drive to the lodge for dinner. The sounds of music and laughter grew louder and louder. Then a loud crash as the boat hit the breakwater at high speed. I ran along the shoreline to find their boat sinking but the passengers laughing and splashing about, by and large unharmed. Sometimes I got the feeling that God protects those who imbibe. But why?

Although many a young woman had overnighted on Ed's cruiser, none were allowed in the guys' sleeping quarters. Were they allowed, they'd never have accepted the invitation. Ghastly things took place down there. It was no place for young women, or anyone really with a decent upbringing. For example, there were flammable flatulence competitions, which, I'm embarrassed to say, are highly entertaining to the unsophisticated.

Around three forty-five each afternoon, a bunch of us would walk together up the hot, black asphalt road to the lodge for the evening shift. If I was going to work as a bellhop, I'd have on a starched white shirt that would be soaked with perspiration and wrinkled by the time we reached the top.

On occasion, we'd break into song, making it up as we went along, a line sung by one of us, the next line by another and so on. It occurs to me now that those songs were akin to those sung by chain gangs laying railroad ties.

Fourth of Ju-ly...
Think that I'll fry...
Cuz it's hotter than hell...
In the Ozarks...in the summer.

Makin' a dollar a day, boys,
Makin' a dollar a day
Boss has a yacht and a Caddy
What more is there to say?

Turns out the girls had their own song (sung to the tune of Elvis's "Heartbreak Hotel"):

Well, since Ed Popkess called me,
I found a new place to dwell,
It's down at the end of Lake Ozark,
Arrowhead Lodge!

I'm makin' a dollar a day, boy,
Makin' a dollar a day
I'm makin' a dollar a day, boy
All the time!

The bellhop's tears are fallin'
The desk clerk's dressed in black

They been so long at Arrowhead
They never will get back.

The waitresses are a-runnin'
Their squaw skirts drag the floor
Their silver belts are clankin'
As they run through the door. [1]

Ed Baskett's [2] *always complainin'*
He says that life is cruel
So last night when the clock struck twelve
We threw him in the pool.

The waitresses would also sing "Waltzin' My Hoover" (to the tune of "Waltzing Matilda") as they vacuumed the dining room floor.

* * *

The girls roomed in one of two places. One was unfortunate; the other, even less fortunate: windowless rooms on the ground floor that they sometimes referred to as The Dungeon, with no lamps, only bare bulbs on the ceilings. This was where first-year girls stayed.

---

[1]   Sometimes sung as "As they pull up their drawers."

[2]   Ed Baskett was an easy-to-tease bellhop from Sabetha, Kansas.

There was a dark, narrow passageway behind the rooms that served as a closet and a path to a small bath. "How many girls did the bathroom serve?" Ellen, a maid, asked today. "Too many."

Annie also lived in a room off the tunnel. As did Glen, cohabiting at least one summer down there with his wife.

Oddly, most Dungeon girls recall their summers down there rather fondly. "We laughed all summer," said one. "We had cigar parties. We found all sorts of ways to be obnoxious."

* * *

Having put in their time in The Dungeon, those who returned for a second year were customarily promoted from house-keepers to waitresses and were upgraded from their zero-star accommodations to, well, one star? The She Shack, a cottage out the back door of the kitchen, behind the trash barrels. Occasionally, a waitress walking to the Shack would be struck by refuse carelessly flung out the rear kitchen door. Marilyn, for example, was hit by a wine bottle.

The two-room She Shack cabin comfortably accommo-dated four. But six to eight were crammed into the front room on bunk beds. The back room was a communal closet. They had to part some hanging clothes to get to the tiny, moldy bathroom. "You could sit on the pot, wash your hands, and take a shower all at the same time," Gina, a waitress, recalled. No air-conditioning, just a fan. "Makeup would run down our faces as we tried to make ourselves presentable for work."

"Sometimes we'd find out what air-conditioned guest rooms weren't occupied and we'd sleep in them," Marilyn recalled. "A couple of times they forgot to alert us when they rented the rooms. There were surprises."

Chapter Eight

Amateur Night in the Kitchen

Chef Glen

Most of the chefs and cooks I met at the lodge seemed to drink a lot—maybe it's the heat—and, on occasion, go nuts.

One drunken night Chef Glen decided to go to Hawaii, not

an easy thing to do from Lake of the Ozarks. He got Slugger to drive him to Jeff City and from there flew—with any number of plane changes—to Honolulu. He debarked, walked to the nearest airport shop, bought three Hawaiian shirts, and flew back to Jeff City. The shirts looked like ones I'd seen at Kmart but the man was a slave to authenticity. Which is not to say he didn't just buy them in Jeff City and lie about going to Hawaii.

When he was drunk, he was most often a belligerent drunk. He got into altercations. His weapon of choice, what with being a chef and all, was a butcher knife. Never used it, he just liked to wave it in the air, to *wield* it.

One such altercation was domestic in nature. Glen, stark naked, chased his wife down the basement hallway. A witness said she was laughing as she ran.

Wouldn't you know it, a guest called the front desk to complain about the noise. The next morning all paying guests on that floor checked out, as did Glen's wife. Last anyone heard, she was living in a small bungalow in California, but living.

Another instance involved state liquor inspectors. During the dinner hour, two of these plainclothes liquor cops came in and observed a waitress placing cans of beer in the ice maker. This was said to be illegal, but why? And do we really need to pay these guys to make absolutely sure we're drinking warm beer? Where were the framers of our Constitution on this one?

The inspectors went into the kitchen to announce they

were shutting down the dining room. Glen begged to differ. He picked up his trusty butcher knife, wielded it, and chased them out of the kitchen, the dining room, the lodge, and the parking lot. Never saw or heard from them again. It was the Ozark way.

Other times, the altercations had to do with employee relations. "I witnessed, more than once, Glen going after [desk clerk] Jim Robinson," said Ina Kay, a waitress. "Jim used one of those big metal trays as a shield like a gladiator in a Roman battle. One of those times Jim got in a shot himself and coldcocked Glen near the lobby fireplace. Glen lay there unconscious practically the whole night." Turned out Glen was unconscious an estimated 10 percent of the summer.

Boofie Sinclair operated the Jayhawk Cafe on campus in Lawrence, Kansas, and spent summers cooking at Arrowhead. He drank copious amounts of Ten High, every day. He was a funny, spunky, pugnacious guy who once very nearly got into a fight with Wilt Chamberlain, a tall student-athlete at Kansas who called to tell him he'd forgotten his hat at the Jayhawk and told Boofie to bring it to him.

That may have been the only time that anyone said "no" to Wilt, who then said he was coming right over to get his hat and to kick Boofie's butt—no small threat coming from a giant. "How will I know you?" Boofie asked the world-famous seven-footer. Luckily Wilt, with his busy superstar's schedule, never found time to drop by.

Jim Murphy, who married Boofie's daughter, Sandy, a waitress, was a cook who drank scotch and water from goldfish bowls at staff parties.

Bill Tillman, a hurdler on the Kansas track team, was not what you'd call an alcoholic, but he worked in the kitchen, always with a beer in his hand. At a staff party on Horseshoe Bend he was egged into trying to jump over a Volkswagen. He did, but slipped on wet grass when he landed and broke his wrist. When a doctor put his wrist in a cast, Bill had him fashion a custom indentation that would hold a beer can.

Annie Hicks was the hardworking head cook. She always wore newly stained kitchen whites and always had a cigarette in her mouth. Sara worked in the kitchen and still pictures Annie mixing salad in a huge bowl with her hands and arms, a bit of her cigarette ash falling from time to time into the salad. No one complained.

Alcoholism may have skipped a generation in Annie's family, leaping o'er her and making a direct hit on her son, Howie. He showed up one day, a bus dropping him off right in front of the lodge. Annie was surprised to see him.

He said he'd been working for NASA on "the moon project," but had to quit because he had heart surgery. Using Annie's pull in the kitchen, Howie was hired and made a smooth transition from the Apollo program to dishwasher.

He chose not to party with the help. Rather Howie went on his own to bars that catered to locals. For a variety of reasons related to alcoholic beverages, Harry landed in the Miller

County jail in Tuscumbia on several occasions. When he didn't show up for work for a couple of days, Ed would dispatch Pete to spring him.

Pete would drive up to the jail in Ed's big white Caddy convertible, top down, creating quite a stir in the small town. Was Howard Hughes or Elvis or Marilyn Monroe in their local jail?

Pete let folks wonder. He smiled and waved and walked inside, posted bail for Howie, and was directed to cells in the basement. And there was Howie all right, his cell unlocked and the door open, a forerunner of the minimum-security confinement concept that would later become popular throughout the nation. It would have been a pain in the ass to go down to unlock the door to feed him three meals a day, let alone cook them. So prisoners were allowed to leave, walk up the street to the local café, charge their meals to the county, and return to jail.

Just so you don't get the idea that they coddle criminals in Miller County, the jail cell was filthy and there was a rat or two running around.

But Glen was the chef and team leader of the kitchen drinking brigade. He led by example. When he was AWOL he could sometimes be found at the pool, not sleeping it off on a chaise lounge but completely passed out on the concrete deck, face up, arms folded across his chest, as if laid out for visitation in a funeral parlor. It was disconcerting the first time you saw it, enough to make you call an ambulance if there'd been one. There wasn't.

This could have serious consequences. One such viewing of Chef Glen by the pool occurred just before the restaurant opened on a busy night in August.

We tried to shake him conscious: "Glen, Glen, gotta get up. Time to go to work."

"Like hell," he murmured, without opening his eyes, which was highly unprofessional, I thought.

"What'll we do now?" I asked.

"Whadaya mean 'we'?" Jim Murphy replied. "Looks like you're the chef of the day."

All of Glen's backups were off that night for some reason, which was not good. Yikes! Who's running this place? Untrained personnel would have to fill in on an emergency basis. Me and Wheez.

Wheez had worked a couple of breakfasts and was okay on scrambled (not over easy) eggs and toast. But dinner? On what was expected to be a very busy night?

My own cooking experience was pretty much limited to Kraft macaroni and cheese, which at nineteen cents a box saw me through college.

"Shitfire!" was Annie's response when we broke it to her.

Just thirty minutes into dinner hour, the kitchen took on the air of a Civil War battlefield triage unit with hustling and bustling and bumping and yelling and spilling. Annie hotfooted about in her white apron splattered with beef juice and chicken blood that made her look like a sawbones just out of field surgery.

"Where's my medium-rare steak order?" yelled a waitress.

"Not gonna happen," I said, shaking my head, trying to break it to her gently. "Poor thing never had a chance."

She looked at Wheezer for a second opinion.

"Didn't make it," Dr. Wheezer said. "It's charcoal." Dead meat. Cremated.

"Annie!" I shrieked. "Your chicken's been in the fryer for about half an hour!"

"Shitfire!" Annie responded and searched the boiling grease for the remains.

"Hush puppies don't go on a prime rib platter!" a waitress scolded. "And this is not au jus," she said, pointing to a small plastic container of the brown liquid that accompanied a slice of prime rib. "It's soy sauce. Maybe maple syrup."

"Close enough?" I queried. She shook her head "no."

"Jesus, Wheez, you cut that prime rib three inches thick!" I said.

"Gentleman's cut," he replied, laughing at what was no laughing matter.

"They asked if it was for the whole table," said the waitress who served it. "And I think they were serious."

"Where the *hell* is my lobster?" yelled a waitress. "Got a table's been waiting almost an hour!"

"Shitfire!" remarked Annie, who was in charge of broiling lobsters.

"Pickup! You got three orders sittin' up here!" Wheezer shouted.

"This baked potato doesn't have any potato left inside the foil," commented another a waitress, sounding like she was at the end of her rope on this amateur night.

"Just tell them their potato is being served PE," said another.

"What's 'PE'?"

"Previously eaten," was her answer.

"Is there a salad under that whole bottle of Thousand Island dressing?" Annie snapped.

"Feel free to kiss my ass!" Sarah the salad-maker retorted.

"And there's eight shrimp on that shrimp cocktail."

"Yeah but I only gave the last guy three," Sarah explained.

"Is my Ozark trout up yet?"

"Don't say 'Ozark trout.' Save it for the menu. It's frozen from Germany."

The last customer of the evening came in and ordered prime rib with mashed potatoes.

Wheezer, who had been under duress for several hours, snapped: "Mashed potatoes?! Who the hell orders mashed potatoes with prime rib?"

"We're eighty-six mashed potatoes," I said, adding flames to the fire. (86, in kitchen parlance, means "completely out.")

Then, Wheezer had an epiphany, a vision of mashed potatoes, the last place he'd seen mashed potatoes. Somewhere, but where? It was here! Suddenly he flew out the back door and down the steps to the big trash barrels. He opened one. No spuds. A second, nope. But in the third Wheez struck mashed Yukon golds! He spooned some up, raced back up to the kitchen, and slapped them down on the plate next to the prime rib. The waiting waitress gave him an are-you-serious? stare but served it.

After the dinner hour had passed, one waitress summed up the evening: "We survived. But I don't think we picked up any repeat business."

Uncle Ed promotes Wheezer.

Chapter Nine

The Great Salad Bar Debate

Annie

*T*he times they were a-changin', and Annic Hicks didn't want any part of it.

"Shitfire" (her favorite expression), said old, gray-haired Annie, wearing her besmirched white apron, leaning on a kitchen counter, a cigarette dangling from her lips. "Glen brings some of the craziest durned ideas back from California."

Annie was his sous chef, if you will, who for years worked long days on her feet in Arrowhead's kitchen and showed it. She was in the back, doing food prep most of each day, then cooking lobsters and fried chicken during dinner hours.

"One time his big idea was 'broasted' chicken," Annie told me. "I said, 'Glen, what in the goddamned hell is *broasted* chicken?'

"We was always knowed for good chicken," said Annie, who spoke in the Ozark hills vernacular. "And I didn't see no need to mess with it." It was also something of a slap in the face to Annie, who cooked all the chicken.

Glen told her that "broasted" chicken was the hottest new thing to hit the West Coast. "He thinks any crazy newfangled thing they come up with in California is the cat's vagina," Annie said.

"You mean the cat's meow?" I asked.

"Glen always says 'vagina,'" she replied, although she may not have known what the word meant. "Pete told me it was 'cat's vagina.'"

Glen was a wordsmith, all right, who'd recite poetry, largely to himself, but loud enough for the rest of us to hear, while he toiled in the hot kitchen. One of his favorites:

May the bleeding piles torment you,
May corns adorn your feet.

*May crabs as big as cockroaches crawl around your balls
    and eat.*
*And when you're old and feeble, and your mind's a total
    wreck,*
May you fall right through your asshole,
And break your goddamned neck.

Beautiful Glen. Hate to admit this, but I laughed. I was no poetry scholar, but I thought it was pretty good.

And in the early sixties, it did seem all things new and exciting were emanating from Southern California. Everybody was moving there or acting as if they had. Kids in landlocked Iowa were listening to the Beach Boys' "Surfin' USA," wearing baggies and black Connies (low-cut Converse All Stars), and dyeing blond sun streaks in their hair. It was, like, totally gnarly. (They weren't wearing "huarache sandals" like the song said, because they'd ask for "Archie sandals" and storekeepers didn't know what they were talking about—didn't know what huaraches were either for that matter.)

So, Annie, what culinary advance, what revolutionary concept in dining had Glen smuggled out of California this time?

"He called it 'the salad bar,'" she said. "Never heard of it. What the goddamned *hell's* a salad bar?" Her first question to Glen was the same one she'd posed about broasted chicken.

"Glen said it was like a buffet but only for salad," Annie said, recounting their at times testy Q and A re: salad bars.

Annie just plain didn't get it.

A salad buffet? Back then folks could only think of a couple salad ingredients. You had your lettuce, dressing, maybe some tomato.

"People go to the salad bar and make their own salads themselves," Glen explained.

"What do you mean 'make their own salads'?"

"Just what I said," Glen had replied.

"Why would any damned fool want to do that?" Annie queried. "What's wrong with salad the way it is?"

"Because," Glen had answered, "you can make it just the way you like it at a salad bar. In California they've got lettuce, cherry tomatoes, radishes, carrots, chickpeas, beets, croutons, cucumber, olives, broccoli, green pepper, cauliflower. They grow everything right there.

"Oh," Glen continued, "and hard boiled eggs, chopped up bacon, cottage cheese, potato salad..."

"So you're a-tellin' me folks got to get up out of their seats at their table and go make their own salads?" Annie asked in disbelief

"That's it," Glen replied.

"Well shitfire," she told him. "The whole idea of goin' out ta eat is so's other people do the work for ya. Do ya give 'em a dollar off for makin' their own salads?"

"Nope," she recalled him saying. "In California they think it's fun. Something different instead of the same old thing."

Apparently, Glen had done a heap of thinking on this subject, salad bar psychology. Which was not really like him.

He told Annie something to the effect that people in California want to be individuals, do their own thing, make their own salads. Not just eat the salad put in front of them and in front of everybody else everywhere they eat.

"Was that what he was saying?" I asked.

"Somethin' like that," Annie answered.

"It sounds as though he stopped just short of saying the Bill of Rights guarantees citizens the right to pursue happiness by making their own salads, their way."

"It's stupid," she said. "What next? A wash-your-own-dishes bar? And what's to keep some big fat guy from eatin' everything on the salad table?"

"Small plates," Glen said. "And you put up signs: 'No Sharing' and 'No Seconds.'"

"You'd have to keep a close eye on 'em," Annie cautioned.

Glen said he'd maybe have Noble, the muscular handyman at the lodge, monitor the situation. Glen wound up asking Noble to build him a salad bar. Noble didn't want to and kept putting it off, putting it off.

Over time, Janet caught wind of Glen's big idea and nixed it. "I didn't want our waitresses having to explain the whole concept and procedures to customers," she said. "I didn't want customers wandering around the dining room. I didn't want to take out three tables to make room for the damned thing. And I didn't want to see Noble tackling customers who went back for seconds, with dressing and lettuce flying all over the place. With him, a rule's a rule."

97

"This ain't California," Annie reminded Glen. "This is Missour-a."

* * *

Years later I was involved in just such a situation during a family reunion in Indianapolis. We were all staying in a Holiday Inn with a country farm–themed restaurant where waitresses wore old-fashioned blue gingham dresses, old farm implements hung on the walls, that sort of thing.

I went down to the restaurant, where there was a breakfast buffet with a small sign: "No Sharing." I joined my sister-in-law, Sharon, who'd already been through the buffet line and was sitting in a booth. As we talked, I nibbled on a slice of her bacon.

A white-haired, grandmotherly waitress sidled up to me, bent down, and said softly in my ear: "I seen what youse a-doin', you little shit-ass."

Chapter Ten

Ozark Bellhops

*T*here may have been "no surprises" at the Holiday Inn down the road but, oh boy, there were surprises at Arrowhead Lodge, all right, with amenities and features unexpected and often unappreciated in these Ozark hills.

At Arrowhead, guests checking in were asked questions they weren't prepared to answer: "Do you prefer the American Plan or the European Plan?"

"What?" they'd reply, and I'd explain that one plan includes meals and the other does not, without confessing that I myself wasn't sure which was which since no one ever chose the one that did.

We didn't ask if they'd be paying with cash or a credit card, because there really weren't any credit cards. Not yet, leastwise not around these parts. ("You mean to tell me you just sign your name and they give you stuff?")

Puggy, the chief desk clerk, would next say, "Billy, our

bellhop, can help you with your bags," and they might reply: "Billy our what?"

Bellhops. In the Ozarks?

"I can handle them myself," they'd say, or words to that effect, but usually too late, after Puggy had handed me their room keys so they couldn't gain access without me.

The keys themselves added to their state of confusion. Aunt Janet, tired of replacing room keys that parting guests forgot to return, had attached them to full-sized rubber tomahawks adorned with feathers.

By this point, the guests were rattled. For most this was their first interaction with a bellhop. We were probably the only ones between St. Louis and Kansas City. We wore uniforms of sorts: white shirts that we'd spray starched and ironed ourselves— hence the occasional brown burn marks of a rookie. Worn with black pants and black bow ties, the outfits weren't elaborate to be sure but enough to suggest that we were hotel employees, not members of some luggage-snatching gang that hung out in lobbies, as some guests suspected.

We lunged for their bags, like monkeys at bananas, which startled and scared people, frankly, who hailed from mid-Missouri towns like Moberly and Versailles (the latter pronounced in American, exactly as it appears here).

If their luggage was still in the car, I ignored their insistence that they could fetch it without me, marching purposefully by their sides out to their cars. I might chime in with some chummy remark, commenting on the beautiful day (95 degrees with

80 percent humidity) or asking: "Where you folks from?"—to establish a bond, to ingratiate myself.

This could backfire, like the time I noticed a license plate holder that read "Parkhill Motors, Champaign, Illinois," and I chirped enthusiastically, "Hey, I'm from Champaign!" whereupon the man snapped, "You are?!" slammed down the trunk, and sped off with his passenger, an attractive blond woman some thirty years his junior.

Once in a blue moon, a dad would walk in with luggage in hand and—Ding! Ding! Ding! Ding!—an attractive young daughter in tow.

I'd step in front of him, blocking his path to the front desk, grab at the bags like a purse snatcher and ask in a rapid-fire blur: "*Sleepwithyrdawtertdayfryasir?*" just to see if I could pull it off. Dads would reply. "That's okay. I'll can do it myself," or words to that effect.

Girls were always on our minds. More so, I would say, than boys were on girls' minds. And certainly with more prurient interest. Why couldn't we even up the hormone levels between the two genders so at least we'd all be on the same page?

Occasionally a couple of unaccompanied girls would check in together. Ding! Ding! Ding! Ding! I'd see them to their room, then hustle back to the front desk to punch "off" the circuit breaker for their air conditioner. In seconds, their light on the bulky, aged black switchboard would glow and I'd push in the plug.

"Hello, front desk," I'd say. "How may I be of service this afternoon?"

"Our air conditioner doesn't work," one of the girls would say. "We're hot." Indeed.

"Place cool washcloths on your chests... necks, rather... I'll be right there," I said with a sense of urgency and was off to the rescue. Sometimes I'd pick up John along the way because he was handsome. (It was my strategy to hang out with handsome guys, thinking they'd attract a lot of good-looking girls and I'd have a shot at some of the decent-looking leftovers. This didn't really work, either.)

Our response time was pretty much dependent on the Hotness Index of the damsels in distress, the index based upon their physical attractiveness and "approachability." If their Index reading was high, we might pick up a toolbox on the way. For credibility. With these two girls, we went that extra mile, stopping in the supply room to pick up a big, heavy, black, iron... thing, who knows what it was, and rolled it into their room on a hand truck.

"What's that?" asked the blonde, slim-yet-somehow-still-curvy-with-the-face-of-an-angel.

"Sweet Jesus," I thought to myself as I admired her, but apparently murmured audibly.

"What?" she asked.

"This?" I replied. "Oh this. This is the... the Kool-More, the Kool-More 5000," I said, adding, "Would you like to come to our staff party at the pool tonight?"

"I think we're going to the Ozark Opry," said the brunette, who made Natalie Wood look like the Wicked Witch of the East.

While they discussed their options for the evening, John and I draped wires randomly from their air conditioner to the big, heavy, black, iron thing and started making electrical sounds such as "Bzzzzt, bzzzzt" and the like. We looked at each other and burst out laughing. The girls were puzzled.

"I think we got 'er!" I said proudly, then ran out of the room, up the stairs, hit the circuit breaker, and bounded back down to their room, breathless. "Working?" I asked.

"Yes!" said the brunette. "We can't thank you enough."

Well, actually you could, I thought, but settled for "Just happy to help out."

They said "yes" to the pool party after I reminded them that the Opry did shows every night, failing to mention that our pool parties were also held on a near-nightly basis. In the hallway, John and I gave each other a smile and would certainly have given each other a high-five if such a thing existed.

The pool parties could get raucous. Ina Kay, a waitress, remembered a dishwasher who jumped off the fire escape thinking he was jumping into the pool but fell forty yards short, landing on the stone patio. And lived. She also remembered the night another waitress, Van, was tossed into the pool and her falsies floated to the surface. Boob jobs were still in the development stage.

About ten, our two girls with the air conditioner problem, the Goddesses of Ladue, strolled out to the pool, looking even more ravishing than before.

"Wow," said Richard, more mature than John and me, a

smooth, handsome ladies' man from Kansas, who also bested us in status as one of the day desk clerks. Naturally, I began to worry.

But the two girls came straight to us, giving thanks once again for saving them from heatstroke. We spent the entire evening fetching them cold beers and acting fascinated with whatever the hell they were talking about: mascara, miniskirts, whatever it took.

And after all that, when they became tipsy and decided it was time to duck into the shadows and make out...it was not with us.

With Rich? No. Worse. With each other!

Damn! Ever hear of such a thing? Oh, sure, you have *now*. But in the early sixties? And these were *attractive* girls! They didn't have to resort to such desperate measures.

I thought that after all the time and effort and beer we'd put into our relationships...this unrequited lust was terribly rude.

Was the world changing, or were these two just plain nuts? I hoped it was the latter. I certainly didn't need *more* competition, did I? Jesus.

We didn't have much experience with the likes of Them. Well, there was Mike, the son of Zoolena Ferguson, who ran the gift shop, but Mike was sort of *beyond*...He was tall and heavyset, like an NFL lineman, except he was given to wearing colorful, patterned muumuus with sandals that looked like he bought them at Bob's Women's Wear for Men. The muumuus billowed as he swished dramatically through the front door, making his entrance into the lobby as though coming out of the wings to take center stage at the Metropolitan Opera House. He was a drama king to be sure, sounding like Nathan Lane in *The Birdcage* even when he was merely ordering a tuna salad sandwich. Mike's account of a trip to Carl's Market to buy lunchmeat was as dramatic as Homer's *Odyssey*.

I don't recall any whispers or snide remarks about Mike's proclivities. Funny about these Ozark folk, these presumed rednecks. You never heard racial slurs or nasty remarks about sexual preferences (beyond the occasional "light in the loafers"). Not the way you would in far more cosmopolitan St. Louis or Chicago. Now, you *would* hear Baptists badmouthing Methodists.

* * *

There would be further disappointments that summer on my journey to erase the ugly scar of virginity. As a young man you were made to feel like there was something terribly wrong with you, especially since most guys lied about their ages the first time they had sex by two, three, four, or five years! I felt like I should be wearing a scarlet "V." I thought at one point that I had lost my virginity on Ed's boat, only to look it up in Webster's and find that, strictly defined, I had not.

A pair of older (mid-twenties) women checked in, experienced an air-conditioning malfunction and asked Wheezer and

I during our repair call if we'd sleep with them. Knocked my socks, and pants, off! We didn't even know their names, and I suspected they didn't much care about ours, but guess what? We weren't offended in the least.

I probably should have known this was too good to be true. There was something in the matter-of-fact tone of their request—as if they were asking for extra towels.

Still, we couldn't whip off our black bellhop slacks fast enough. The women stripped to their underwear and looked mighty fine doing it if I may say so. There were two single beds so it wasn't immediately clear who would sleep with whom. But there would be no losers here.

Or so we thought. We slipped beneath the sheets and turned off the lights. At intervals, I'd hear Wheezer's "date," saying sweet nothings: "Go to sleep, now, let's go to sleep." My "date" was less vocal, physically warding off my advances by scooting toward her edge of the bed. She might have fallen off the edge to the floor but the room was too small. She was just sort of smashed up against the wall, worrying about splinters.

What the hell was going on? Could they be a couple of strict vocabulary-ists? When they asked if we'd like to "sleep" with them could that have been *precisely* what they meant?

In the morning, we woke early, dressed quickly, and were headed for the door when my bed partner stood, kissed me on the cheek, and said: "You were a perfect gentleman."

Great.

* * *

Bellhops were expected to "sell" the rooms. Ed would call from home about four o'clock each afternoon to snap: "You full?" And you'd better be.

Families would typically pull up in front of the hotel and send Moms in on reconnaissance missions, which often included seeing the rooms before they signed.

The rooms on the first floor were the last to go. This was euphemistically called "the garden floor," probably because of the green fungi, algae, molds, and various other scums thriving in the dank bathroom corners.

"Do you smell something?" a woman might ask as we walked down the hall. "No, ma'am," I said firmly and falsely. "I don't. Maybe it's that new cleaning fluid the maids are using." I was walking cautiously, not wanting to slip on the sweating linoleum floor. "Or it could be my pine forest aftershave."

Looking inside she might next comment on the room's coziness. "It's so small." And indeed occupants of the two beds could sleep holding hands.

"There are three of us," she'd say.

"You know," I said, charmingly, thoughtfully, placing my hand on my chin, "it's funny. Four people stayed here for a week with a rollaway between the beds, and they loved it."

That was ... not true.

"Sounds good," she said. "I'll go get my family."

And neither was that. Never saw the big, fat liar again.

* * *

The lake did not attract a well-heeled, cosmopolitan crowd. Rather, a lot of decidedly small-town, middle-class folks— and cheap you might say—who didn't quite *get* tipping. Most had never used the services of a bellhop. They would tip waitresses, however, the standard 5 to 10 percent.

So, when I was carrying worn American Tourister luggage from a family's Ford Falcon to their twelve-dollar room, I sensed that it was going to be like wringing blood from a stone.

You could see it in their blank looks after I set the bags down in their rooms. Early on in my bellhop career, I'd just walk out the door and curse the cheap bastards. But over time I learned not to give up. There's always something more you can do.

I'd launch into a routine to give them more time to *think*: "Let me check to see if you have enough towels [more time], plenty of soap [more], the air conditioner is working properly [more], the TV [more], the lamp is functional [c'mon!]...the pool is down the hall and out the door [you're killin' me over here!]. The restaurant is open for breakfast...lunch...and dinner [even more]. If you need anything [idiots] my name is Bill, I'm working here this summer to make some [friggin'] money for college! [You stupid hayseeds!]"

If none of that worked I'd fold my arms across my chest and stare at them until hell froze over.

August, when the lodge was always full, was the best time for tips. A bellhop could go home with twenty dollars in tips from the day. But a couple of summers, right in the middle of August, a Purina animal feed mini-convention descended on the hotel and tipping pretty much came to a halt except for a few dimes and nickels. These were super hicks, people from small towns or no towns at all. We had to wear Purina red-and-white checked shirts. My dreams turned to nightmares when I saw those red-and-white checks in my sleep.

But we always had that dollar-a-day to fall back on.

* * *

Another role played by bellhops was protecting Puggy from assault by rightfully angry tourists. We released reserved rooms at 4:00 p.m. if the reservers had not shown up. Occasionally, we overbooked, so it became necessary for Puggy and me to set the lobby clock ahead from 3:45 to 4:00 p.m. Then sweat it out.

When the front door flew open at the real 3:55 p.m. we knew all hell was about to break loose. You could tell people had been driving like crazy to make the deadline. They were rattled. And sweaty.

The dad would step up to the desk and say, "Whew. Made it. I have a reservation."

"What's the name?"

"Shitoutofluck," he'd say, or should have said.

"You're Shitoutofluck?" Puggy would reply.

"Yes I am."

Puggy would leaf through the reservation book, looking in vain for what, I did not know, but she appeared to be doing her level best to help.

"I'm sorry, Mr. Shitoutofluck, I'm afraid we released that room at four o'clock."

"But it's 3:55!" Shitoutofluck howled.

"Our clock says 4:05," Puggy said pointing at the little hands on the little clock. "Sorry for the misunderstanding."

"Do you have another room?"

"No, Mr. Shitoutofluck. Not for tonight." And that was the truth. All forty-one rooms were rented and soldiers from Fort Leonard Wood had paid a nominal amount to sleep on the floor in the supply room

"Get me another room, close by. And nice!" he snarled.

"I'm afraid the closest vacancy would be in Jeff City," she said, delivering that news softly, sweetly, gently. Then, Shitoutofluck would glare at me. At that moment he wanted to kill somebody with his bare hands and it might as well be some scrawny, pimply-faced, little jag like myself.

Chapter Eleven

The Pow Wow Room

The Pow Wow Pub had been the utilitarian, largely unused, no-real-purpose Pow Wow *Room*, until Uncle Ed magically managed to obtain a liquor license.

Previously, if dining customers wanted an alcoholic beverage they had to bring their own, then order "setups," which were mixers, such as tonic, seltzer, Coke, or a glass of ice—paying almost as much for the setup as they'd pay anywhere else for the drink itself.

For certain favored customers, a waitress would take their drink orders and pass them along to Jim Chappell, who would duck down behind the front desk and do the bartending sight unseen. Ed wasn't selling alcohol but figured there was no law against giving it away. Was there? Probably too late to do anything about it now.

I didn't get it. People said it had something to do with Southern Baptists. Turned out lots of things around there did.

The Pow Wow Room was a plain, wood-paneled...room... furnished with a couple of rough-hewn knotty pine tables and chairs. It had a big old jukebox that contained many hit records, but alas would play but one, C-6, "Cool Jerk," a highly danceable tune by the Capitols that went something like this: "Cool jerk...dah dah dah...cool jerk," and so on. Ad nauseam. Annoying? Yes, yes it was. But some thought it imparted something of a bizarre Zen quality to our parties. Others, like me, argued that, no, it was more akin to the musical weaponry the FBI employed to dislodge criminals in prolonged standoffs when they couldn't take it anymore.

Actually, if you got lucky, there was one other song it might play: "Double Shot (Of My Baby's Love)." Know it? By the Swingin' Medallions?

But, was it enough to sustain an indoor employee party on a rainy evening? Yes, it was, with enough Schlitz and Ten High. The Schlitz was free, which we obtained by pilferage from the back of a beer truck—in moderation, one case per visit when the driver was making his delivery. Somewhere along the way I'd learned not to be piggish when stealing, which I realize is not, like, one of those commandments chiseled in stone, but it's a pretty good corollary.

We thought we were pret-ty sly dogs pulling off the beer caper, but the driver noticed the second time we did it. Ed told us he knew what we were up to and said he should fire the entire three-man gang—one thief, two lookouts. But he didn't. I think what stopped him was the nature of the stolen goods, i.e., beer. He knew we were too young to buy it and damnit! Teenagers need beer. Simple as that.

About the only others who used the Pow Wow Room were big-time country music stars. Legends who'd come up from the Grand Ole Opry in Nashville for gigs at the local Austin Wood's Opry. Austin was blind. We'd see his big Cadillac coming toward us on the highway and always say, "Little more to the right, Austin."

Some of the stars were big, like legendary Roy Acuff, the "King of Country Music," and Ernest Tubb, a pioneer of country music whose stature was completely lost on us. Odd, then, that I can recall every word of some of his hits, like "I'm Walkin' the Floor over You."

That was back when country music was purely by and for country folk, with yodeling, thick, syrupy, almost unintelligible accents, twangy slide guitars and fiddles. There was no country music radio north of the Mason-Dixon Line. Way before a scantily clad runway model from Canada doing crossover could be classified as a "country singer."

Here, in deepest Missouri, you could hear the hard stuff on your radio: "How Can I Miss You When You Won't Go Away?," "Dust on the Bible," "I've Got Tears in My Ears from Lyin' on My Back in My Bed While I Cry Over You," "Drop Kick Me Jesus (Through the Goal Posts of Life)." Loved them all. The titles.

The Nashville stars would come back to the Lodge after a show, some still sporting rhinestone-encrusted jackets, looking like they'd been dipped in glue and rolled through the precious stones department at Woolworth's.

They'd hang these weighty, bedazzling garments on the backs of their chairs and proceed to partake in straight, room-temperature Kentucky and Tennessee bourbons and straight five-card-stud poker late into the night. We could watch, but not from directly behind them. They didn't want our facial expressions to tip their hands. There were no groupies and no cursing.

One memorable night, a staff party was raging in the Pow Wow Room and in walked Roger Miller with his guitar.

He sang all his big hits—"King of the Road," "Dang Me," and "Chug-A-Lug," which we all liked. Wheezer picked up a guitar and, though he'd never picked one up before, accompanied Roger.

Roger, known for his sense of humor, looked over at Wheezer and remarked, "Man, you're good." The Wheez smiled and nodded his head in recognition of such a fine compliment.

"And I've got something new for ya," Roger announced to the group. "A song I wrote on a trip to London. I haven't even recorded it yet. Tell me what you think."

He sang, "England swings like a pendulum do..."

"Whadaya think?" he said.

Well, it was probably his own fault for using rip-roaring drunks aged eighteen to twenty-two as a focus group, but since he'd asked:

"Not good," I heard someone say, possibly Pete, a music

major from Oklahoma. Pete and I agreed it sounded like a jingle written by the London Chamber of Commerce.

And then the coup de grâce, from Jill, a maid and sophomore at Northeast Missouri State University at Kirksville: "You're a dumb ass, Roger!" But he took the feedback well, going on to record the song, which immediately went to number 3 on the country charts.

* * *

How the Pow Wow Room became the Pow Wow Pub, with a liquor license, will never be known, but it may have had something to do with a meeting Ed had with someone in the state capitol building in Jefferson City. I accompanied him on the day trip.

Ed carried a brown leather briefcase. Who knew Ed had a briefcase? He put the Caddy convertible in a parking garage across from the capitol, which cost ten cents an hour. (How did they even pay the guy in the booth?)

It was August. There were about eight lonesome cars in the garage. (Hey! That's eighty cents right there!) The legislature was not in session. No one was around. We walked across the street and entered the capitol by a side door. Inside, Ed said, "Take a look around. You might learn something, El Stupid. Meet me back here in thirty minutes."

The capitol itself was empty except for a tour group of about ten campers aged eight or so on a field trip to learn about democracy and such.

The Ten Commandments were displayed on a seven-by-ten-foot pink-and-gray marble slab.

"Now, who can tell me who Jefferson City was named after?" the guide asked the group of kids. Some of the kids stared at the floor, but a couple of them raised their hands, one particularly annoying youngster jumping up and down, begging "Oh, oh, me." But the guide picked a boy with eyes glued to the floor. "Matt?"

"Jeffer Davis?" he said.

"Good guess, but I'm afraid that is incorrect," the guide said.

"Thomas Jefferson!" the me-me boy answered, correctly. Later the group would walk outside to see a large statue of Thomas Jefferson facing the mighty, muddy Missouri river.

"This capitol building," the guide continued inside, "is where our democratically elected representatives gather to discuss important issues and vote on new laws to improve our way of life."

The children were by and large awestruck, looking up into the soaring and ornately decorated rotunda. It was not unlike an old cathedral.

I watched as they wandered past the Thomas Hart Benton murals depicting the history of the state, somewhat controversial because there was some bad (slaves) sprinkled in with the good.

Ed and I met at the base of the staircase, flanked by statues of Lewis and Clark.

I never asked what his meeting was about and don't mean to cast aspersions, but when I returned the next summer, the

Pow Wow Room had become the Pow Wow Pub. State liquor laws had changed, I was told, to allow somewhat smaller hotels to serve alcoholic beverages—hotels that had forty or more rooms. Arrowhead had forty-one.

Maybe, just maybe, Ed should have been the one conducting that tour back at the capitol explaining to those kids how democracy works.

Pete at the bar in the Pow Wow Pub

Chapter Twelve

La Noche de la Larry Don

The "Larry-Don" Excursion Boat, Lake of the Ozarks, Missouri

I fell in love on the *Larry Don*. But first, I had to get aboard.

It wasn't easy. I was working the evening shift on the front desk while most of my coworkers were already at the dam, jubilantly boarding the queen of all sightseeing boats for a party on its Moonlight Cruise.

The *Larry Don* was an old barge-like vessel, akin to a wide

World War II landing craft, or maybe a scow. But painted up brightly and festooned with strings of colored lights it took on a festive air. At twenty-four-feet wide and sixty-five-feet long, with a second observation deck on the roof, there was plenty of room for a good-sized crowd plus a band. There were weddings on the *Larry Don.*

I was ready to fly out the door to join the party if only this one last couple would just get the hell out of the dining room, which had closed a good half hour ago. The two were sipping wine, laughing, and just generally pissing me off.

I tried to plant a seed by shutting off the lights, something I do only in extremis.

"Hey!" the man howled from their table in the back.

"Sorry," I answered. "Didn't realize you were *still* back there."

Their waitress, Gina, I believe, who had been leaning against the ice machine, arms crossed and scowling, hauled out a vacuum cleaner and began vigorously attacking the carpet near their table. I can't recall if she asked them to please pick up their feet or not, but I like to think she did. Wouldn't put it past her. This was a moment that called for drastic measures.

"Would you like doggy bags?" she asked them almost politely.

Finally, the couple stood up slowly and strolled up to the desk to pay their check.

"Sorry about the lights," I said as I rung up their bill.

"Bullshit," the man replied. "You did that last time."

Guess it was time for some fresh tactics.

The *Larry Don* was by then already leaving the dock down

119

at the dam. But there was a backup plan. The few of us still on duty were to rendezvous with them in the middle of the lake in some dramatic fashion I couldn't quite picture.

Jim Murphy waited for us out front in the lodge station wagon. I jumped in next to a couple of waitresses who'd shed their squaw dresses for more suitable party wear, which could have been just about anything, frankly.

Also along for the ride was a young dishwasher who'd left a few dirty ones behind.

Jim spun the tires in the gravel parking lot and we were off down the dark, narrow, winding road to Ed's dock. Despite being reckless behind the wheel and a heavy drinker, Jim had been given Ed's permission to use the speedboat. Approaching Janet and Ed's house, Jim went into stealth mode, cutting the engine and dousing the car lights.

We tiptoed down the hill, untied the boat, hopped in, and immediately went to work on some six-packs with a beer can opener (see: "Primitive Tools of Early Man"). We idled out to the breakwater, then opened her up, all the way. The bow jerked up and we were pinned back in our seats like aquanauts on blastoff, our wake glowing white in the darkness.

We whooped and hollered, "Wahooooo!" This was exhilarating, about as exhilarating as life would ever get now that I think back on it. The lake was smooth and fast with few boats to stir it.

The eighty-degree summer air felt cool at thirty miles per hour. A sliver moon gave just enough light to clearly show the shoreline but not too much to drown out the fusillade of stars.

We passed the small purple neon cross that marked Our Lady of the Lake Chapel and served as a landmark for night boaters. Then by the high bluffs, where on a previous night excursion we had witnessed a car take a ninety-foot plunge, its headlights beaming hauntingly up from the bottom. We'd rushed to the scene, but neither heard nor saw anything above and saw nothing floating on the surface, dead or alive. Never did hear or see anything about the incident. Weird. Just another unexplained mystery in the Lake of the Ozarks files.

After the bluffs, there was only darkness for a while, no lights to the left along the south shore in those days and few to the right until we rounded the tip of Horseshoe Bend with its small, rustic mom-and-pop spots for families that came for the fishing. Breezy Point, Clem's Cabins, Sun 'n' Fun. No condos yet, no expensive resorts with golf courses.

It couldn't have been more than a Schlitz or two later that Jim shouted: "Thar she blows, mateys! The USS *Larry Don!*"

And what a vision it was, ethereal, slowly towing the reflections of its colorful lights that danced on the inky water.

Jim, not one to be enchanted, was. He turned off the engine and we sat there, bobbing slightly, taking in this apparition. What's more it was accompanied by dreamy music. Not the rock 'n' roll that we relied on at home to transport us to more exciting states of mind. Little Richard, Buddy Holly, and Jerry Lee Lewis were not called for here. The band on the *Larry Don* was playing

"It Had to Be You," a mellow number for slow dancing, designed to make you swoon and sway.

Jim pulled the speedboat alongside the *Larry Don* and tossed a rope to a deckhand. The six of us leaped from the speedboat to the mother ship, into the arms of our colleagues.

They cheered us as heroic partiers willing to do whatever it took.

Dana gave me a big hug and her best kiss yet. "You did it!" she cried. "What an entrance!"

The band played "Put Your Head on My Shoulder" and couples on the dance floor melted into each other's arms.

Dana and I climbed the stairs to the second deck. We sat and hugged in the summer breeze, in the moonlight that glistened on the water. And I fell in love. With love. With having someone to hold. With the summer breeze, with the moonlight. With that moment. All of it.

Chapter Thirteen

Sisterhood of Servers

Waitresses

We were all coming of age and learning about life, and a most unusual life-form it was at Lake of the Ozarks. Many of us did wonder if what we were learning had any application to the outside world. Kind of like guys who "Join the Army and Learn a Trade" and wind up learning how to fix malfunctioning tank treads. You never see want ads for that position.

Marilyn probably had the greatest adjustment and the most to learn. She was a Missouri farm girl, raised as a strict Southern Baptist, and, at just sixteen years old, the youngest of the summer staff. She was hired in a housekeeping emergency when someone quit unexpectedly.

She said except for going to school or to the store, she'd only left the farm once on a day trip to St. Louis, I worried that she'd think life at Arrowhead Lodge represented life in the real world. When I asked how things were going she said, "I've seen things I'd never seen before." I braced for what might come next. "I didn't know that everyone on vacation cuts their toenails and fingernails and leaves them on the floor."

"Oh," I responded. She said she was appalled that girls as well as boys could go for months without changing their sheets. She'd seen three girls sneak out of a room where three boys were staying and run down the fire escape. "When we cleaned the room it was obvious there had been some kind of orgy," she said, too shy to share details.

Things like this just did not happen on the farm. She felt she had to tell her parents but worried they'd tell her to come straight home. But when she called them, her mother laughed and said: "Honey, you're finally finding out about the real world."

Some of the guys would try to embarrass her. She was responsible for cleaning the men's room three times a day. And Fred from Oklahoma would go in there, sit on the commode fully clothed, and make grunting and farting noises. "I turned as red as my hair," she said.

Noble the all-purpose handyman/engineer at the lodge would put an electric cord that felt like a snake under her sheets and stand outside waiting for her to scream. "I always did," she said.

One afternoon, after being promoted to waitress, Marilyn was in the She Shack getting into her squaw dress for a dinner shift. Squaw dresses were the waitresses' uniforms, which came in a variety of pastels adorned with glittery golden or silver stitching and cinched at the waist with silver Indian-esque belts. These days this might be called "cultural appropriation," but frankly the dresses weren't close enough to anything ever worn by any Native American to qualify.

It dawned on Marilyn that she was the only one getting ready for work. She walked briskly out to the pool and saw all of her fellow waitresses on floats holding nearly empty bottles of champagne.

When she asked why they weren't getting ready for work they replied, "Work?" At this point, most seemed unsure of where they were or why. They tripped back to the She Shack where some passed out and others took turns driving the porcelain bus.

"Thank God," said Gina, "Marilyn was a teetotaling Southern Baptist. She saved us."

"My mother," Marilyn said, "preached the evils of alcohol as well as other tips on behavior before I came to the lake. She'd say: 'Do with your knees what you please, but keep your thighs a surprise.'"

Marilyn served almost every customer in the dining room single-handedly that evening, aided by a few off-duty bellhops and busboys. A few things even Marilyn could not do. She tried and failed to keep a man and his great Dane from dining together.

"There are AA meetings in the dining room," Marilyn said. "Women tell about getting drunk and lying on their backs looking at the stars with their legs spread. It's amazing what you hear pouring coffee."

The girls, more so than the boys, seemed to have great camaraderie and esprit de corps. Once each summer the waitresses had to remove all the tables and chairs from the dining room to strip and wax the floor, a task that took almost all night. Toolie, Fergie's daughter and a real pistol, brought some kick-ass rock 'n' roll albums (vinyl), others brought beer. Noble volunteered to man the polisher, a powerful, heavy-duty rogue beast that seemed capable of flinging waitresses through the front window onto US 54. "Somehow," said one, "even that turned out to be fun."

There were rites of passage upon entering the waitress-hood. Willis, who was married to Alice, took them on wild rides in his Jeep down the hill through all the rocks and trees and brush. "He drove very fast and the limbs whipped across your face," Marilyn said. "You had to duck and dodge as best you could. He'd hit a log or a deep ditch, slam it into reverse, and back up at full speed.

"We didn't know those woods that well," she said, "but we knew there was a cliff out there and not too far away. It was a hair-raising, pants-wetting, nail-biting, praying experience."

Other rites involved drinking. I advised a few of the younger, inexperienced drinkers that I ate saltine crackers spread with butter before I drank alcohol—"butt and crack"—on my unproven theory that it would coat my stomach and block the absorption of alcohol. Field tests failed to support this theory.

"How did we all get there?" Ellen asked. You had to have a connection. Gina was Marilyn's sister, who was Ina Kay's friend, who was Carolyn's niece, who was brought by a friend, Betty, who was a girlfriend of Ralph Robinson, who was Jim Robinson's older brother.

Willy was Helen's sister. Tom was Gina's brother. Gina and I were friends from Louisiana, Missouri, and we were both freshmen at Northeast Missouri State.

Rich was from Sabetha, Kansas, and Ed was his younger brother. Roger Popkess was, obviously, related to Ed.

Toolie was Fergie's daughter and Dixie was Toolie's friend.

Pat was Ed's sister. Slugger was her son, Bebe was Slugger's sister, Teddy was their younger brother. I was Ed's nephew. Bill, Ed, and Tim (aka Wheezer) were my high school buddies from Illinois.

Blood relatives received no special treatment. In fact they were often first to be fired. Slugger, for example, was fired several times.

* * *

"Ed was a good boss," Ellen said. "He took us out for a party on his cruiser and let us use his speedboat sometimes to go skiing. And he supported us. When guests complained that the employees were using the pool he told them if they didn't like it they could leave." At Arrowhead the customer was not always right.

Ed had a temper. There were heated moments when he threw one or more guests out of "my hotel." A couple brought a dripping watermelon through the lobby and up to their room. Janet thought that was tacky and told Ed to throw them out. The incident ended with Ed saying "Get the hell out of my hotel." He always referred to the lodge as "my hotel" when he got worked up and tossed someone. After the watermelon couple left Ed remarked: "They were probably pretty nice people."

Another time it was an entire convention. The convention-
eers objected to the employees fraternizing with them in the
Pow Wow Room. Ed told them to get the hell out of "my hotel."
He wouldn't let bellhops carry their bags or waitresses serve
them in the dining room. They had to walk, carrying their bags
down the hill to the chapel to catch a bus.

On another occasion, Ed was summoned to the hotel, which
violated one of his cardinal rules: Never bother him at home.
He barged in the front door and yelled, "Who the hell wants
to see me?"

The complainant was sitting at a table in the lobby and
identified himself.

"What the hell do you want to talk about, pal?" Ed queried.

"First of all—" the guy began.

"Hold on," Ed commanded. "'First of all' means you have a
lot of complaints and I haven't got time to hear 'em all."

Then he dropped the hammer. "Get the hell out of my hotel
and don't come back."

Now, Ed could also turn the tables and fire the staff, all of
it. Ina Kay said he once had to close the hotel for two weeks
for lack of employees and never did that again.

But he would fire the same employee multiple times. Ina
Kay for example.

"He fired me at least three times," she told me, "the first
time for being left-handed." Workplace discrimination laws
did not address left-handedness, not to mention there may
not have been workplace discrimation laws of any kind back

then. Chef Glen firmly believed that carrying trays left-handed "looked funny" and caused accidents.

"I was fired a second time for dropping a steak knife in Janet's lap," Ina Kay said, which Ed treated as attempted murder. The third time, Glen didn't feel like broiling a lobster five minutes before closing time and Ina Kay had to deliver the bad (fake) news that the kitchen had run out of lobster.

"You're fired!" Ed yelled at her. "We're never out of anything when it comes to our year-round customers."

She never left, a strategy that seemed to work.

You could often tell when Ed was about to go off. He would hang out in the lobby, drinking and loudly greeting people coming in for dinner. The mood was generally jovial, but when you heard him address someone as "pal" you knew there was trouble. Usually it was in response to some criticism of the hotel or an employee.

Ed would twitch and say something on the order of "If you don't like it, why don't you get your ass out of my hotel, pal?" Then he'd turn to skinny-ass me, skinny-ass Pete, and skinny-ass Chappell and say, "Boys, throw this joker out of here!"

The three of us would look at each other as if to say "Us?!" The joker would look at us as if to say "Them?"

At that point, there wasn't much we could do. I had once threatened to call the police, knowing full well there weren't any. Another time I took the malcontent aside and explained to him, sotto voce, that Uncle Ed was upset because he'd been diagnosed that afternoon with stage four brain cancer.

"Really?" said the guy, stunned by the news.

"Inoperable," I replied.

* * *

There was upward mobility. "Somebody left and I was promoted to kitchen duty," said Ellen. "I was thrilled. The kitchen is where all the action is, and where all the people are. I peel potatoes, make salads, wash dishes, and do whatever Annie tells me to do.

"She's a tough old bird. One morning after an evening of drinking adult beverages, I was late to work with a horrible hangover. Annie gave me my punishment. I had to clean the grease traps beneath the sinks. The smell was overwhelming. I've never been late again."

Many of the waitresses appeared no bigger, nor heavier, than the trays they carried. Such was the case with young Marilyn.

One morning as Marilyn went through the swinging kitchen door, a pitcher of warm syrup tipped and poured down her chest, "between my little boobs," parting in three streams down each leg and into her underwear. About eight breakfasts hit the floor. "The entire dining room erupted in laughter," she said. "I had the sweetest pussy in town."

Marilyn! What would your mother say?

She was probably the sweetest girl around already. She even befriended the grouchy old night desk clerk, Jim Teague. "We shared eggs in the morning," she said. "He liked yolks.

I liked whites." She drove him to Jeff City to buy shirts. "He was color-blind and needed help. He wrote me letters of encouragement while I was in college. I still have them."

Old Teague asked her to accompany him to a room where a guest was freaking out. Teague wanted a witness. "A woman was shaking and crying and begging for 'one more drink' and grabbing hold of my dress and wouldn't stop," Marilyn said. "Noble finally gave her enough booze that she passed out and he drove her to some clinic in Kansas City."

Fergie, who ran the gift shop and whose full name was Zoolena Ferguson, would ask Marilyn to go to Eldon to wire money to her daughter, Toolie, who had a baby girl but no father around. Marilyn did this for Fergie several times, always on the sly because Janet did not approve.

On top of everything else, the waitresses always had Glen to contend with. With a slap of a spatula he'd yell at them for making the salads or the shrimp cocktails too big: "Girls! We're feeding these people, not trying to fatten them up for slaughter!"

And his "jokes"! He told the same ones every day, like the one that was something about a blind man walking past a fish market and saying "Ethel, is that you?" Get it?

Sexual harassment in the workplace, you say? Creating a hostile work environment? We didn't have names for stuff like that back then. Just some real dumb-asses to put up with.

Chapter Fourteen

I Don't Get It

The 1960s were times of change. Most places. Not so much here. And in some respects not even yet.

Martin Luther King Jr. and the Freedom Riders were demonstrating in the South for the right to sit at lunch counters and wherever they pleased on buses.

But Missouri is not really the South. Or North. Lake of the Ozarks had no segregated lunch counters or buses—not because Ozark folk are more tolerant, there just weren't any "others" to be tolerant of.

There were no black or brown people that occurred naturally, or by any other means, at the lake. No blacks, no Hispanics. So it was a tough place to be racist. Telling a racist joke about them would have been like telling a joke about Reykjavikians.

Missouri was a border state. There were slaves in Missouri a hundred years before, but even then they were few and far between, especially in central Missouri, which was way too rocky and hilly to grow cash crops.

Being from St. Louis, Janet and Ed knew about racial discrimination and civil rights.

"You know what you do if black people come in?" Janet asked the table of us folding napkins before the dining room opened one evening. I held my breath. "You seat them just like anybody else. They'll probably be testers looking to be turned away."

And so it was, one evening when I was the desk clerk, an older black couple, best dressed couple in the Ozarks, came in for dinner. They were the only black people I saw in eight summers at the lake.

"Good evening," I said as they walked past the desk toward the dining room.

"It's the *best* evening," the man said emphatically. "You ought to pop your head out and look at the stars."

The hostess showed them to a table for two, a "deuce," at the front of the dining room about fifteen feet from where I stood. A few customers did turn to look, but no murmurs swept the restaurant and no one walked out.

"How's the prime rib?" the gray-haired man asked Marilyn, their waitress.

"Excellent," she said. "We're known for it."

"It's rich and salty," said the woman who was with him, apparently his wife. "Your doctor wouldn't like that choice. Bad for your blood pressure." I think it's bad for cholesterol too, but no one had heard of cholesterol yet.

He ordered it anyway.

"I noticed later that he was picking at it," said Marilyn, "and so I went over and asked him if it was all right. He said 'yes' it was, but as I walked away I heard a loud thud. I turned around and the man had fallen off his chair and was lying on the floor."

Someone from the next table hopped up and loosened the man's collar and tie. We didn't have mouth-to-mouth resuscitation, no CPR, no Heimlich maneuver, 911, no EMTs back then.

A couple of men picked him up and carried him past the desk to the nearest room, 212. His wife's hand gripped his— their two hands firmly clasped as they must have been at the altar a lifetime ago. At first shocked and sobbing, she now bore the look of someone who knew the worst had happened. His face looked that way to me, like the faces of my grandfathers as they lay in their caskets. After they'd passed, I stood staring down blankly at the desktop. I'd never seen anyone die. And now the man who minutes before had smiled on his way in and told me to go out and look at the stars would be leaving, dead. I was so glad he'd seen the stars.

Someone suggested I call the proper authorities, but I couldn't imagine who that might be. There were no hospitals, clinics, doctors, EMTs, not even a cop anywhere around here. Eventually an ambulance from somewhere arrived.

It was a busy night in the dining room and within ten or fifteen minutes, the couple's table was reset and a much younger couple sat down for dinner. They smiled when the hostess gave them their menus.

I was shaking my head slowly from side to side, when Ed asked, "What's the matter, Billy?" I glanced over at the table.

"Life goes on," he said.

"I don't get it," I replied. Still don't. I remember the night my dad died. I walked around the neighborhood saying "I don't get it" over and over.

Call it "the circle of life" or "part of life" or whatever you like, but I've had a lot of years now to think on the subject and witnessed death and lost many friends and loved ones, and you know what? I still don't get it.

I took a moment away from the desk to go out and get a breath of fresh air. And admire the vast, majestic, bejeweled night sky. I think it helped.

Chapter Fifteen

Night Desk

Ol' Jim Teague, probably about seventy-five years old, was the overnight desk clerk. Came on about 9:00 p.m. He'd sit behind the front desk for about an hour, doing nothing, then move to a comfortable chair nearby where he would continue to do nothing until he dozed off.

He offered little in the way of security, but this was back when we didn't worry a whole helluva lot about security. We didn't have surveillance cameras, gated communities, home security systems, microwave movement detection systems, car alarms, card scanners to gain entry to work, guns on our nightstands, and politicians and security firms that tried to scare us into voting for them or buying something. Robbery of course was always a possibility, if not the probability news channels would have us believe. I don't buy free-floating fear. I never bought The Club, that antitheft steering wheel bar I've seen on an old orange Pinto with a Blue Book value of an open bag of Cheetos.

One night while Teague slept, Jim Murphy and Noble Needham picked up the cash register, carried it downstairs, then woke up ol' man Teague and asked him for change for the cigarette machine. (A pack was thirty-five cents, and boy did people bitch about that.)

"Get it yourself," Teague mumbled.

"The register's locked," Jim reminded him.

Teague rose slowly and fumbled for his keys as he shuffled over behind the desk. He found the key but...no register!

"Jesus Christ!" Teague yelled. "Where's the goddamned register?"

"You're in deep shit," Jim said, shaking his head. Then he and Noble burst out laughing.

* * *

Nights at the front desk were usually quiet, but did have their moments.

A young couple was spending their wedding night at the lodge when midway through it the bride came sprinting down the hall and through the lobby screaming "I married a monster! I married a monster!"—apparently not the abusive variety but the kind who makes nutty requests. As the groom checked out the next morning, alone, he was asked the standard question: "How was your stay?"

* * *

Then there was the Night of the Mad Hungry Man Last One Standing No-Holds-Barred Missouri Death Match.

Teague and I were sitting in the lobby when a loud, burly, belligerent drunk crashed through the front door, yelling "Restaurant open?" It sounded less like a question than a demand.

"No," Teague answered, with what may have been a bemused what-a-stupid-question lilt. "It's been closed for way over an hour." I half expected Teague to add: "Stick around, it reopens for breakfast in eight hours." Teague did have that grumpy old man way about him.

"We're hungry!" the man hollered.

"Not open," Teague said curtly.

Hungry Man, as he forever came to be known in lodge lore, grabbed frail, old Teague by the collar, pulled him to within an inch of his face and shouted, "How about now?! Now is it open?!" Then he shoved Teague hard against the wall.

I don't like bullies, never have, a half century before it became a cause. Also, I have a temper, having always been told it's because I have red hair. My high school buddies remind me of the time we were walking down the street and were confronted by some toughs, one of whom pulled a knife. I responded by pulling my jacket open, sticking out my rather unimpressive chest, and challenging our would-be assailant: "Go ahead! You haven't got the guts to use it!" I guessed correctly. (Thank you, Jesus.)

Aunt Janet displayed some of her gift shop wares in

the lobby, among them a large, rather heavy two-by-three-foot green plaster statue of Buddha sitting sideways on an elephant.

Unbeknownst to Hungry Man, who was still occupied with Teague and with his back turned to me, I picked up that symbol of peace, love, and harmony, and brought it crashing down on his head. This substantially loosened his grasp of Teague's collar and sent Hungry Man slumping to the floor, stunned and momentarily unconscious.

Someone, I think it was Pete, yelled, "You killed him!" But Hungry Man stirred, came up in something of a kung fu pose, then hit the floor again before crab-walking sideways on all fours out the front door.

The next morning, Ed asked Pete, "What the hell happened here last night?"

And Pete replied: "A man came in, asked if the dining room was open, and Billy hit him over the head with a statue." Thanks, Pete.

* * *

Occasionally, another old timer, Bud, an old friend of Teague's, would stop in late in the evening for a cup of coffee and some reminiscing.

He'd grown up in Linn Creek, a small town nearby that had to be moved uphill or torn down, lock, stock, and barrel when the dam was built and the water came in.

He said everything between 628 feet above sea level and the 660 feet of the lake's surface had to be demolished by fire or dynamite: houses, barns, schools, trees, churches, bank, gas station, store. All that remained were tree stumps and piles of broken concrete. "Cemeteries, too, yeah," Bud said. "Some of the cemetery crew quit.

"People cried, watching their town go." He said the town of about four hundred was close knit. Families intermarried. Everyone knew everyone else. "If there was a lost cow wandering through town, everyone knew whose cow it was."

He said many people had their houses pulled up the hill to the new Linn Creek or the new town of Camdenton. He added that as the water was rising, lawyers were still working feverishly on land deals with local folk. "They'd taken over the biggest house in town for their offices and when they moved it uphill the lawyers just stayed in there working." Bud chuckled.

Teague asked him if he'd tell me the story about his grandmother. And he said he'd be happy to.

"I was fourteen," he said. "My folks said for me to go over and check to see how Grandma was a-doin'," he recollected. "As I was a-walkin' up to her house I seen a man climbin' out of a truck who I was pretty sure I'd seen before, someplace. He was wearin' dirty clothes. He was with another fella who was wearin' a clean white shirt and a necktie and shiny shoes. They walk up the front steps and shiny shoes knocks on the door. Grandma answers it and the man says,

'Mornin', ma'am,' he says, tippin' his hat, all polite-like, like he was sellin' Bibles or somethin'. 'I'm with the 'lectric company.'

"'Figured,' she says, talkin' at him through the screen door.

"'Well,' he says, 'water's risin' and we got to get you folks safely out of here so's you don't drown.'

"Here he is, actin' like he's here to rescue people when he's part of the cause of the whole thing. The flood."

"'Might as else come on in then,' Grandma says. Man says he can't stay but a minute because the two of them are right busy. And they were all of that.

"The dirty clothes guy stays on the porch. Inside Grandma is tellin' the 'lectric man I'm her grandson. He says his name and offers his hand, but I don't take it, just give him a little nod.

"He opens his case, takes some papers out, hands 'em over to Grandma, and starts spoutin' a bunch of mumbo jumbo about what she has to do to get the money for her house. But we can't really follow what he's tryin' to say. Had the feelin' he liked it that way.

"Grandma tells every bit of our family's eighty years in this house—since before the war between the states. Weddings at the house, and menfolk comin' home from wars, and the big ol' oak tree in the front yard that she'd watched grow practically from an acorn.

"She shows 'lectric man a photograph of a man she says was my great-granddaddy, an Osage Indian, with long black hair.

He wasn't none too happy about white folk a-comin', and he let 'em know it, Grandma says. The Osage was fierce.

"Anyways, after about a half hour of family history, there's a rappin' on the door and the dirty clothes guy steps inside. He's been waitin' on the porch, spittin' tobacca juice over the railin', tappin' his foot, and swattin' at flies. He makes no greetin's and grunts to 'lectric man: 'Gotta get to it.'

"'So we got to leave now, I reckon,' Grandma says.

"'Water's risin',' 'lectric man says. 'Got your things ready?'

"'We have everthin' boxed up cause we knew you was a-comin'. We heard what you're here to do. Most of our things are in the wagon.'

"'Lectric man helps with the loadin', I guess to show he was halfway human.

"Grandma steps out the front door for the last time, wearing her Sunday-go-to-meetin' dress. She pays no mind to what's goin' on around her, not lettin' anythin' bother her, the way she'd had to do her whole life, carryin' on with a stiff upper lip, through floods, droughts, two children dyin'. She won't give the 'lectric men no satisfaction.

"She wraps a red shawl round her shoulders, raises her chin, and walks slowly down the steps like a queen. She takes my hand to pull herself up onto the wagon seat, her royal coach.

"She looks down at the fella in the dirty clothes, sayin', 'Could you do us the kindness of waitin' 'til we're over the rise before doin' what you come to do?'

"'Yes ma'am,' he replies, tippin' his cap.

"'Let's get a-goin',' she says, and I snap the reins. Tears come to my eyes and I ain't ashamed to say it.

"'Be a man now, boy,' Grandma snaps. 'Don't look back.'

"I think the fella in the dirty clothes probably didn't have to do much, just spread hot coals from the fireplace on the wood floors. Probably all that was needed."

Chapter Sixteen

The Ozark Outback

Turning off US 54 onto State Road 42, the scenery changed suddenly and dramatically, from a thin veneer of roadside tourist claptrap to real, raw, hillbilly country. They didn't call it Lake of the *Ozarks* for nothing.

I always thought the name kind of held it back: a scenic lake 129 miles long back then with 1,375 miles of shoreline, more than the coastline of California, yet few outside the state had ever heard of it.

Road signs were riddled with holes from shotgun blasts, sending a message to outsiders that local folk did not respect the authority of whoever it was that put up those signs, and that somebody else was in charge here. Or nobody. And that's the way they liked it.

There was no law enforcement. Lake Ozark wasn't even a town until 1965.

Used to be you could shoot somebody and if you beat the

police to the state line, well, case closed. By the early sixties, not all that much had really changed in that regard.

Jesse James and his gang used to call rural Missouri home. The civic-minded complained that his robbing and killing gave the entire state a bad reputation and kept businesses from coming here. It didn't help that Hollywood kept reminding the world by making one Jesse James film after another

Darryl Zanuck's 1939 blockbuster film *Jesse James* starring Tyrone Power, Henry Fonda, and Randolph Scott was shot here. The film crew stayed at Arrowhead Lodge. In a famous scene, Jesse and his brother, Frank, jumped of a cliff into the lake on horseback. One horse died. It was then that Hollywood added this pledge to filmgoers: "No animals were harmed in the making of this film."

These days, locals liked to tell the story of a dead body being found in a large-load dryer at the laundromat. Nobody seemed in much of a hurry to find the perpetrator. "Prob'ly had it a-comin'," some said.

Two state police officers were not so much dispatched as moseyed down from Jeff City. Somebody had to remove the body. There just weren't enough dryers for people to use as it was, let alone tying one up for a homicide investigation. They didn't wrap the crime scene in that yellow police tape they have now because they didn't have it back then. No DNA evidence yet either. No forensic crime units. No *CSI*, no *CSI: Las Vegas*, no *CSI: New York*, no *CSI: Miami*, no *CSI: Cyber*. Nothing.

Police didn't really launch an investigation; they just took a gander at the situation and called it quits. After a couple of days, with no leads, they ruled the matter a probable suicide, leaving open the question, if anyone had bothered to ask, of just how the victim managed to keep feeding quarters into the slot as he tumbled inside the dryer.

Family members of the dearly departed said not to worry about the jurisprudence aspect, they'd handle it. Local justice was faster and probably more on target than that dispensed up at the courthouses in Tuscumbia or Versailles.

The area had a long history of locals taking law enforcement into their own hands. In the 1800s unsavory characters fled the law in populated areas, coming here to the boondocks to steal from the settlers, especially horses, cattle, and hogs. They also became adept at counterfeiting, producing bills so true to the real things that huge amounts were accepted for large tracts of land.

The settlers formed vigilante groups known as "slickers" from their unique way of dealing with criminals, who they tied to trees and "slicked"—whipped with hickory branches until they vowed to leave the area. As can happen with vigilantes, the slickers got carried away and an "anti-slickers" group was formed to combat their excesses.

* * *

In the 1960s, traveling inland on the country roads, away from the lake, you saw old, dead refrigerators out on rotting front porches, alongside couches and chairs that were meant to be indoors but were out there in the elements hemorrhaging white stuffing. (In an effort to polish its image, one North Carolina town I visited for CBS had banned "illegal porch furniture," i.e., indoor furniture on front porches. Tacky.)

Continuing down Route 42 you saw a few scrawny chickens— "racing chickens"—strutting through weedy front yards adorned with one to five rusting hulls of long since immobile automobiles. Old, graying unpainted barns leaned leeward. Trees were blanketed with heavy gray webs woven by some sort of industrious pest that was out to kill them.

The first town you came to was Brumley (population: 87). There were tarpaper shacks that had collapsed, some replaced with mobile homes a few feet away. There was a bar across from a stucco Baptist church. Nearby was a New England–style white frame Christian church with a green plywood addition. It was decorated with fake stained-glass windows, plastic stuff you buy in rolls. The Honey Springs Baptist Church was in a double-wide trailer. These towns seem to have plenty of churches and beauty salons like Pat's Beauty Charm and Ruth's Beauty Shop, if little else.

You saw signs announcing the Brumley Lions Club shooting match and ham and bean dinner in September. The Shell Station screen door had a Holsum Bread screen guard and a sign reading "It's Kool Inside." There were decals on the windows advertising Pioneer chainsaws, Beech-Nut Chewing Tobacco, bait and tackle. The landscaping featured old tires painted red, white, and blue planted with roses.

I was on an off-the-beaten-path Voyage of Discovery with Danny, my tour guide, the twenty-something son of Puggy, the desk clerk, and Noble the Jack of all trades who kept the lodge running. Noble liked to egg you into saying things disparaging of local folk. "You could have went and gone to Harvard U-ni-ver-si-ty and it don't mean you're smarter than me. Better than me. Throw you in them woods and you'd starve to death."

"Probably," I'd answer.

Danny generously offered to take me on a field trip to a local backwoods bar. Local in terms of distance, but very far from the world as I knew it.

As he drove, he thought it a good idea to lay down a few ground rules, "to be safe." Probably more instruction and preparation than I received before going on patrols in Vietnam.

"Don't talk politics," he said, "which you may not even think of as politics but could be taken that-a-way. These folks aren't real fond of politicians of any stripe. Fact is, they probably couldn't name any.

"Sports are tricky," Danny said. "Pretty safe with the Cardinals." (No Royals yet.)

"Religion's worse." Danny drove in silence for a bit, before adding: "Prob'ly best if you just don't say much of anything...

"...to anybody.

"And don't order any pussy drinks," he continued.

"Like what?" I asked.

"No gin and tonics," Danny explained.

"Stick to beer. Falstaff. Or a Stag. You like Stag?"

"Probably," I said. They were all the same to me. Except for Coors. People would drive from the Midwest to Colorado and back to buy cases of Coors.

We pulled up to a little, almost shedlike building with two small unlit signs reading "Bar" and "Beer." There was a sheet of plywood where the front window was supposed to be.

Before we went in, Danny passed along a few more tips for the health and well-being of strangers in rural taverns:

"Don't look at the women, if there are any. Probably shouldn't look at the men either. Just look down into your beer.

"And don't play the jukebox. Good way to start a fight."

"Really?" I replied as we walked inside.

"Really," Danny said.

"How ya doin'?" Danny said to the bartender as we walked in. "What happened to yer winda?"

The bartender said a guy played something nobody else liked on the jukebox and was thrown through the window.

"Must have been a pretty bad song," Danny said.

"'Red Sails in the Sunset,'" the bartender said.

"Wasn't that by . . ." Danny started to say.

"Pat Boone," the bartender said, finishing Danny's sentence.

"Got what he deserved," I wanted to say.

"It was late and the guys got a little frisky," the bartender explained.

"Wow!" I said. "That must have hurt."

"Not as bad as bein' thrown through plywood," the bartender said with a chuckle.

Danny and I took seats at the bar next to a big jar of what? Body parts? Hooves? Toes? The bartender could tell I was baffled and said "pickled pigs' feet." Never had the pleasure. I suppose I should have had one, the way you're supposed to eat sparrows on a stick in Chinatown. To honor their culture. But I was concerned about regurgitation.

Small crowd. Danny knew a few people. They avoided talking religion and politics—which I frankly didn't think any of them were prepared to do. They talked about their dogs. I stared in silence at my beer bottle. I didn't talk. I had cats. Pussycats.

One guy's name was Wayne. "So, what are you doin' here?" he asked in a somewhat threatening tone, made all the more so by his drunken slurring. But I don't think he meant it that way. It was just that outsiders rarely came here. Fair question. Who would come to this shithole?

"You on vacation?" he asked, eyeing my polo shirt and Weejuns as I eyed his scuffed cowboy boots and the once white T-shirt he'd altered by tearing off the sleeves.

"Naw," I said trying to pick up the vernacular. "Workin' over at the lake washin' dishes."

Should have said "warshin'," but I seemed to have defused the situation, holding a job even those in his social stratum wouldn't really want.

I met a nice taxidermist. He specialized in small furry animals: chipmunks, skunks, rabbits, and the like. "I won a contest with one of 'em," he bragged, pulling out his wallet to show me a photograph of a prairie dog standing on his hind legs wearing a straw hat and a bandana.

Another feller was tellin' about goin' fishin'. Did he say somethin' about dynamite? Yes he did. "Dynamite fishin'. Never heard of it?" he asked

"Don't reckon I have," I replied.

"Where you from?" he asked, trying to get to the root cause of my ignorance. "The big city?

"Simple," he said. "Toss a stick of dynamite into a pool or stream where you think fish are at, it stuns 'em, they float up, and you scoop 'em with your net. Sometimes you'll blow 'em to bits and you can't eat 'em."

I almost said, "Maybe on little crackers" but I didn't.

The bartender's friend, Tiny, who was about three hundred pounds, came over. "Shoot some pool?" he said. I wasn't sure if this was a question or a command. I was pretty good at pool back then and Tiny was drunk so it seemed like a good idea...until 1 reconsidered my being good at pool and my opponent being drunk and weighing three hundred pounds.

He handed me a cue that was broken in half, probably over some unfortunate's skull, and stuck back together with black electrician's tape. It didn't hold together for long and I played most of the game with a two-foot cue.

Tiny beat me and settled our bet on the game for "a six-pack plus one."

"One what?" I asked.

"One more six-pack," he guffawed.

Plus, a couple shots of moonshine, white lightnin', homemade hooch distilled just out the back door. He found it in his heart to share a couple of fingers with us. The ultimate sign of hillbilly hospitality. "This is the good stuff," Tiny was proud to say.

Ugh! Nasty! Tasted like something you might use to clean the oven and burned like the broiler.

I choked and whinnied like a horse. Danny and Tiny laughed at my rookie reaction. They'd hoped for the best and got it.

"'Nother?" Tiny asked graciously.

"I'm good," I coughed. "Thanks."

"No, here, take it," Tiny said.

"Very hospitable folks in this neck of the woods," I said. I downed it in a single gulp and shook my head violently from side to side as though hooked to a car battery.

I stumbled back to the car. My Voyage of Discovery was over.

* * *

A few summers later I had my second tangle with moonshine, also in Missouri, at a trailer park soiree outside Columbia. Our host was similar in stature to Tiny, large enough that when he walked over to greet folks at the front door, the trailer listed.

Upon opening the door, he looked shocked by my long curly red hair. He had a big, nearly bald head with a small patch of Butch Waxed short hair on top. In those days that put us in opposing cultural camps.

If you had short hair, the long-haired adjudged you to be dumb as a rock. If you had long hair, the short-haired adjudged you to be a flaming communistic homo looking to get your ass kicked.

Our host allowed us in, but only after his wife told him he had to because she worked with my wife, Jody, and had invited her.

White lightnin' and grape juice was served. Purple Jesus. About an hour into the festivities, the projectile vomiting commenced, inside and outside the trailer. Three women in the bathroom were doing synchronized upchucking in anything porcelain: sink, toilet, tub.

Just as I did after my first experience, I staggered to the car. But this time I was driving. Jody couldn't. She was opening the passenger side door and barfing—every quarter mile or so. I worried that someone would toss a cigarette butt out a car window causing the entire highway to burst into flames.

I was experiencing tunnel vision, a descriptive term for this white-lightnin' symptom that causes your field of vision to shrink to that of a soda straw. To see if there was any oncoming traffic I had to steer toward the left lane and hope there was not—although in my condition I really didn't care.

Chapter Seventeen

Getting to the Point

Some nights the staff pool parties crossed the highway and slid downhill to the lakeside.

Revelers moved slowly, single file, toting beer and other necessities, safari-style, trailblazing over stumbly-stones, through briars and brambles and bushes, to a rock outcropping that jutted out over the lake, perfect for diving. A bit higher than perfect if you were sober, which applied to but a few. This was the Point.

Two in the party had flashlights on this dark night, the others rammed into the person ahead whenever the expedition halted unexpectedly

Obviously, we took parties seriously. This was way more of an outdoor survivalist adventure than anything I'd experienced in the Boy Scouts. As remote as it seemed, there were signs of human presence. Marilyn walked right past a naked couple "wrestling" in the bushes that didn't so much as pause in their grappling.

A few waitresses had started this parties-at-the-Point custom years before, in the late fifties. They collected fried chicken from trays returning to the kitchen with the explanation that they were going to have a "picnic."

They didn't want to divulge the real purpose of their venture: skinny-dipping, potentially a real crowd pleaser, for cable or the Olympics. If word got out of naked young women swimming, young men were sure to follow.

I should know, I was the first. I was fifteen or sixteen at the time.

I'd broken their code when I heard two laughing over not needing to worry about bathing suits. I trailed them at a safe distance and took up a vantage point behind some bushes.

But were they really going to *do* this? Right before my very eyes?

Here goes! After chugging a few beers they began stripping off their outer layers.

But how far would they really take this?

Suddenly I saw legs and breasts and backs and necks— better than any bucket of chicken.

And for those of us without sisters, what would real girls look like? Anything like the airbrushed goddesses in *Playboy*? Or would they more closely resemble that aging beauty in the tent at the county fair? You remember, the one with the large appendix scar across her bulging belly? Paid fifty cents (student rate) and that seemed high.

Suddenly, two of the girls stripped completely naked, dashed to the rock, and dove in.

Wow! I had never seen *real girls...girls that you know*, you know? In the flesh.

There was a bit of nervous laughter, I think just because they were actually doing this. They didn't seem particularly self-conscious at all.

What was going on? Were they exhibitionists, sinners, art aficionados, teasers? I could never figure girls out.

It seemed as natural as little sisters taking a bath together. As I watched them diving from the rock, swimming, laughing, it occurred to me they were doing it for *fun*.

Boys would not do this for...fun. Boys would be overwhelmed by their surging hormones and chase after them. I took a deep breath. "They're naked," I told myself. "Get over it." Like paintings and sculptures at an art museum. You don't see art aficionados with bulges in their pants and drool on their chins as they contemplate Gauguin's bare-breasted Tahitian girls.

Yet, this *was* different. There was Renoir's *Young Girl Bathing*, all canvas and paint. But here was Sadie, the real thing, in the flesh, cavorting. Alluring and *alive*. But, alas, no more accessible.

Transfixed, I wasn't paying proper attention to my precarious position. Loose rocks underfoot gave way and I slid from behind the bushes.

"Who goes there?" one of the girls called out as she wrapped herself in a towel.

"Billy?" another queried.

"It's Billy," one confirmed. Others laughed, seemingly relieved that it was just young Billy.

"C'mon, join us."

I wanted to run but it was too late. So I stripped to my underwear—as far as I could go—and walked toward the rock.

"Noooooo!!" they shouted

"Skinny-dip! Skinny-dip!" they chanted.

I was horrified. I flashed back to swimming lessons at our local YMCA, where boys were made to swim nude. Girls wore suits. What!? Why? Years later, the Village People had an answer.

We didn't like it. Young boys standing with their hands folded just so in front of themselves, making sure their eyes never met those of another, as completely clueless instructors explained the easy-to-remember ten basic steps of learning to swim.

Consequently, I didn't learn to swim for years. Our mothers would drop off Ricky Piper and me for swimming lessons. We walked in the front door of the Y and out the back.

We went downtown and walked around, which was kind of an adventure for young kids out on their own. On the return trip we stopped at the fountain in West Side Park and dampened our towels.

And here's one I can barely believe myself: our junior high school, Edison, had a swimming pool. Swimming class was required. Boys swam nude there, too. What's the deal?

It was horrifying. Water, as you know, causes a certain amount of shrinkage, and, I can tell you, so does unwanted public attention. Same with turtles.

So I stood before the girls at the Point wondering, *What will they think? Will they laugh and point?*

I whipped off my shorts, sprinted to the rock, and took the plunge. The girls cheered. A few snickered. I didn't ask why.

* * *

Years later at the Point, at a coed party (with suits) we huddled around a small campfire, hugging whomever was closest. Three beers in, I put my arm around a soft, cuddly, and warm housekeeper who was nothing to write home about, but I didn't see her jotting notes about me to her friends and family, either.

Just then, Phoebe walked over, bent down, and whispered in my ear: "You can do better than that."

"What?!" I said, too loudly. No girl had ever uttered such suggestive words to me, and I never expected to hear any such from her.

So, this is what it's like being cool.

After getting Jean another beer, which seemed like the least a chivalrous man would do—the very least—I was off lickety-split with Phoebe.

We walked up the hill to the highway, then down the dark, winding road toward Uncle Ed's house. We tiptoed past the guys' quarters and down the hill, where we boarded Ed's cabin cruiser, a favorite spot for spooning, and I mean that in the most lascivious sense. We proceeded to the sleeping spaces in the bow.

We frenched. We wiggled around for a full twenty minutes before we both realized we had reached *that* moment, the moment when the foreplay clock runs out. Now what? Your move or mine? The first of many "Now what's" I would experience in the coming years

I was frankly afraid to make any advances. Even though she had been the agent provocateur in all this, I feared she'd turn me down. Or maybe laugh.

Who knew what girls were thinking?

But I did have one trick left. You may have already guessed it. Mental telepathy. Don't scoff, I've seen it bend spoons.

I pressed my forehead against hers and chanted silently but very intensely: *Let's do it! Do it! Doooo it! Now!* ...

I wasn't getting through to her. I altered the pitch, the wordage, the frequency.

For whatever reason, mental telepathy wasn't working. No better than cruising the Steak 'n Shake drive-in hamburger joint on Friday nights, where we never spoke to any girls, never got out of the car, just cruised and tried to look cool. We hoped they'd notice and that we'd wind up making out with them— maybe in a park or somewhere. Unclear.

This did not happen. Ever. Never worked.

Both Phoebe and I finally realized that nothing was going to happen between us, be it her reluctance or mine.

And once again, she whispered in my ear, "It's late. I have to work breakfast tomorrow."

The End.

Chapter Eighteen

Cross-Cultural Exchange

Pete was named, perhaps by me, to head our Cross-Cultural Summer Exchange Program, whereby those of us here for the season would get to know and better appreciate the customs and values of local peoples.

Pete was from Oklahoma. Where? "Blackwell, near Ponca City," he explained when we first met.

"Oh yeah," I replied.

Returning to the boys' quarters late one night I found him in bed with the lights on, a sheet pulled up to his neck, and quivering. He pulled back the sheet to reveal bloody lacerations on his legs.

"What happened?"

One of his cultural exchange attempts had gone terribly wrong.

One of Pete's regular tasks was to drive the station wagon— "Arrowhead Lodge" splashed large on both sides, like a moving billboard—to Stu's Icehouse and Bait Shop to pick up ice every couple of days during the hottest, busiest part of the season when reserves ran low.

Pete was an affable sort, an able ambassador, and once there he'd smile and try to engage the staff in pleasant conversation. But the icehouse gang was a tough—inbred?—crowd. They didn't change expressions nor speak actual words.

Except Gayle, Stu's improbable daughter—adopted?—who was rather attractive and sociable. She and Pete became well acquainted one particularly hot summer when much ice was needed. They corresponded—in writing—several times during the off season and the next summer decided to "do the deed," as he described it, thereby advancing the cause of closer relations with the local citizenry.

She borrowed her uncle's car, Pete brought the beer (Schlitz, hot off the truck), and they drove to the Grand Glaize Drive-In, arriving at dusk just in time for the feature film. He did not recall the title of the film. They did not go to the snack bar or play on the swing set.

Within minutes each chugged a couple of beers and soon found themselves—odd way to put it—in the back seat. Things were progressing quite well when there was this banging on the rear passenger-side window. It was then that she uttered those worst of all words in such a situation: "It's my dad!"

Stu!

And he was accompanied by her even lesser evolved uncle.

These were burly men who tossed around heavy bags of ice like they were throw pillows all day every day.

Somehow, Pete was able to grab his shoes and undershorts and escape through the rear driver's side door.

He ran as fast as he could, obviously, then bounded over a fence so high it kept passing motorists from seeing sinful scenes on the big screen, free. Then he dashed across the road, crashed through a barbed wire fence, and crawled, bleeding, into the dark woods. This is the sort of course that qualifies a soldier for the Green Berets.

Gayle's dad and uncle had seen Pete escape into the woods and now they hunted him. Being hunted in the woods is not good, as any deer would tell you. Pete could see the glow of their cigarettes. Good Lord, they planned to be here so long they had to smoke cigarettes? What next, a campfire? Would he have to trap small animals and eat them?

They came ever closer to Pete before eventually giving up the chase and returning to the drive-in to pick up the car and Gayle. Pete saw this and made for the Methodist parsonage down the road, where he'd try to call the lodge for a ride.

He went to the door wearing only his shoes and undershorts and still bleeding. The minister answered the door and gasped. He wasn't going to let Pete come in. If only his stigmata had been on his palms and feet the preacher might have showed more compassion.

"There's been an accident," Pete said, and asked to use the phone. The preacher was reluctant, but finally allowed

Pete to step inside and make the call. Jim Murphy picked him up.

A week or two later someone from the icehouse returned the rest of Pete's clothes to the front desk at Arrowhead without comment. Jim Murphy, who lived at the lodge year-round, told Pete that over the previous winter someone got into an argument with the guys at the icehouse and was killed!

Henceforth I was sent to the icehouse in place of Pete. The problem with that was Pete and I were both tall, thin redheads. So the first time I went in, the muscular, low-browed men glared at me, then mumbled amongst themselves, apparently deciding that killing me would cost them a good account, not to mention I just might not be the right guy.

Nevertheless, it was a setback for the cultural exchange program and for a greater understanding among peoples in the Bagnell Dam area.

Chapter Nineteen

The Best Laid Plans

$\mathcal{I}$t was already August and here I was, still a virgin. At least according to Webster's.

I decided to launch a two-week initiative to convince A) Dana to go with me to Jeff City and B) spend the night. The overnight was crucial. If that didn't materialize, I didn't really want to go all that way and back on the crazy road.

"Why don't we go up to Jeff City some night and go to a restaurant and a movie?" I asked, wholesomely. Dana balked but eventually agreed.

Then the hard part. Phase two: "By the time we eat and see a movie, it's going to be late. And I don't want to drive back on that dangerous road. So maybe we should, you know, stay overnight."

"Whaaat!?" she replied. "Where?"

I couldn't bring myself to say the word "motel," which back then carried with it licentious overtones. Really. Just the *word*.

The next day, after fabricating my thoughts, I told Dana that

I had a friend who lived up there with his parents in a big house and could probably put us up. She didn't ask how many rooms the two of us would be occupying per se.

"Will his parents be home?" she asked.

"Yes," I answered, although it concerned me that she wasn't getting it.

On the big day, I was off duty at 4:00 p.m. and Dana was off after lunch. I'd asked Ed if I could borrow the lodge wagon, which was never a good bet, but when I told him why, he immediately said, "Yes!"

And so we set out on our Jeff City adventure. I had a big smile and, thinking ahead, a stirring of the loins. Dana was happy, too. I had to wonder if Lewis and Clark were as excited about getting to Jeff City as I was.

We had the windows down, the radio up, and were singing along to "Surfin' Bird," the classic by the Trashmen: "Well, everybody's talkin' about the bird! A well a bird, bird, b-bird's the word...Papa, ooma mow mow, papa ooom mow mow..." Dana favored "Come a little bit closer, you're my kind of man..." by Jay and the Americans. There's no accounting for taste.

I kept sneaking peeks at her. She was a beauty. I felt lucky. Her father probably kept his farmer's daughter locked in the barn to avoid a stampede of clod-kickers.

We arrived at the movie theater in Jeff City just as *Cleopatra* was about to begin. Pulling out all the stops, I bought a large buttered popcorn. Sure, it was expensive, but I wanted to let her know how much she meant to me.

When the movie was over, we drove to Big Mo's (or words to that effect) Steak House, "Where the Meat's Bigger Than the Plate!" The shrimp in the shrimp cocktails were unnaturally large too, looking like they might have been harvested from water discharged by the cooling tower of a nuclear power plant. The baked potatoes? Footballs. The steaks were very tender and very, very thin, which lead me to wonder if Big Mo might be out back driving a truck over them, back and forth, again and again 'til they'd hang off the plates

After dinner, I went to a pay phone outside and made "a call" to the "parents' home." I spoke loudly, hoping Dana could hear.

"Hello, Mrs. Smith, This is Bill, that friend of Bob's who needed two rooms tonight?...Oh no, really? I'm very sorry to hear that...freight or passenger?...Yes, a motel, that's a good idea...Okay, I'll try the Ramada? Thank you, goodbye."

I hung up and turned to Dana. "Someone died. Hit by a westbound freight. They tried to save him at Jefferson City General but he didn't make it. The house is full of relatives in town for the funeral."

"That's terrible," Dana said. "What should we do?"

"She said the Ramada was nice and fairly affordable."

"No. I meant like flowers or a card," Dana said.

Dana was silent as she got back into the car. I was silent as I drove. We were both nervous. It was like we were on the verge of something very exciting but also frightening and perhaps stupid. Like when a roller coaster goes slowly up and up and you anticipate the thrilling, scary plunge. Unless she hadn't figured out where I was going.

I pulled into the Ramada parking lot about as far from the office as I could. I'd just remembered that we were in a powder blue Ford station wagon with "Arrowhead Lodge" emblazoned in two-foot-high letters stretching from front to back.

"Wait here," I told Dana, who had no intention of getting out.

"Gotta act confident," I told myself. "Checking people in is your job."

"Good evening," said the desk clerk. "May I help you?"

"I'm a salesman in town for the Adhesives Expo," I said. (I'd seen a billboard somewhere.)

I was perspiring heavily.

"Haven't heard about it," the clerk said. (Maybe the billboard was in St. Louis.) "So you'll be here all week?"

"Just the night," I said.

"Single?"

"No, the wife is with me." They marry early around here.

I registered: Fred Butkus, 100 Main Street, Chicago. Then signed the form "Bill Geist." Shit. I quickly scrawled that out and signed "Dick Butkus," throwing family resemblance to the wind.

The form asked what firm I was representing:

I wrote: "Midwest Mucilage."

"Good outfit," I remarked.

The clerk pretended not to be paying attention to any of this.

"Your total is $28.50," he said.

Whew! I thought. I worried that Big Mo might have cleaned me out.

"Your room is 102 right here on the first floor so you can come in through the front door."

"Great," I said, thinking *Ugh*. How was Dana going to get past the desk clerk?

I went back to the car and told Dana. "Ugh," she said.

We had no luggage. Sure sign of trysters. I knew. I was a bellhop.

So we hustled in, looking at the walls, the ceiling, the carpet, anything to avoid eye contact with the clerk.

The key didn't work. "Son-of-a-bitch," I said. "Wait here." So there she was, leaning against the wall in the motel hallway alone, probably feeling like a hooker.

I rushed down to the front desk and back, unlocked the door, and we bolted inside. Dana turned on the TV. *The Andy Griffith Show* was on.

"That's where I grew up," Dana said. "*Mayberry R.F.D.*"

I took two beers out of a small cooler I'd brought along.

Then two more and so on.

"Excuse me," she said, and went into the bathroom. I heard her pee for the first time. Moments later she opened the door and emerged in a short T-shirt and underwear. I'm pretty sure I gasped.

She moved quickly to the bed, pulled back the covers, and hopped in. I stripped down to my shorts and joined her.

We were kissing passionately when she grabbed my shoulders, pushed me away, looked me straight in the eye, and said firmly: "I can't."

What do you *mean* you *can't*?!

"I can't do this."

"Why not?!"

"I'm...Catholic."

"Catholic!?" Where's the relevance?! She's probably a member of 4-H, too.

"How do you guys get such big families?"

"I'm sorry," she said.

"But you must have known..." I said.

"I can't."

"I'll sleep in this chair," I snapped.

"You're sweet," she said.

Sweet Jesus! I thought.

She went to sleep. I could tell by her breathing.

I sat in the chair, my feet on the ottoman, for a good hour or two, in the dark, pretty sure I'd never have sex in my lifetime.

If not now, this night, when?

Maybe next year. Next summer.

Chapter Twenty

Autumn Leaves

A dry leaf scoots across the stone patio, making a scratching sound as it goes, scurrying to exit the summer stage and join those scattered down the hill from summers past.

The light breeze pushing it along feels cooler as dusk settles on this, the last day of summer.

Dana and I sit out by the pool on two old wrought-iron chairs that will need a new coat of white paint next spring. We lightly touch hands, not speaking much in these final hours of a summer romance that seemed most improbable when Ed suggested it back in June. What more was there to say?

It had been a week of goodbyes as the summer staff returned to homes and schools. The girls hugged each other and cried. The guys shook hands and uttered meaningless farewells: "Be good, Billy. Don't do anything I wouldn't do."

Funny about guys and goodbyes in my generation. Whether

171

it was here or after college graduation or leaving Vietnam, we said goodbye and moved on, rarely to write or call.

We'd held a memorial service behind the pool, where we buried Wheezer's red baggies, which he was wearing when he got off the bus from Arizona, and wore all summer, day in and day out and many nights too. Some objected to the service on the grounds that we were burying something alive.

We'd had "Slugger's Smoker," filling room 101, the muskiest room on the "garden" floor, with billowing smoke from several cigars. After Slugger had gone.

There was a piano at the entrance to the dining room, and on this final night someone sat down and played "Autumn Leaves." Ed sang along. It was his favorite.

At checkout time the next morning, guests swarmed Puggy at the front desk—questioning an item or two on their tabs—"Who had the BLT? I never had a BLT"—and then they were gone, back to their offices, homes, and schools. Indoors. And the lobby, which had been abuzz for weeks, was suddenly eerily quiet.

Dana and I were in a teary embrace down in Ed's driveway, He was giving us some space to say our last goodbye. Ed wore a slightly bemused look as if to say he'd seen this scene many times before and he undoubtedly had.

He was talking to his friends, Junior and Kathy, who were here as they often were on the Monday of Labor Day weekends to drive me to the airport and fly me home in their four-seater plane. The three of them laughed a few times about something.

"We'd better get going," Junior snapped, for no apparent reason. There was no schedule to keep, but he seemed a bit uncomfortable being present at our private moment. And it wasn't going to get any easier, dragging it out.

"Parting is such sweet sorrow," Ed said as he put his arms around Dana and me. It's interesting, isn't it? How the perfectly chosen word or phrase doesn't mean shit when it comes to matters of the heart. I'd have far more crushing goodbyes in the months and years to come and no wise or comforting words would change a thing.

I tossed my bags in the trunk and we drove off. I waved to Dana from the back window. We passed the Oaks and other summer landmarks, crossed the upside-down bridge, and turned into the airport. We were the only ones there. There wasn't really any *there* there. No terminal, no runway, just a long unpaved stretch of grass for takeoffs and landings.

Junior revved the engine and released the brake, and the plane began to roll and bounce down the grass runway, the turf rolling past faster and faster until we popped into the air. As we rose, more and more of the lake revealed itself, vast and shaped like the Chinese dragon on the wall at House of Chin restaurant back home.

We passed over the Grand Glaize Drive-In, and I couldn't help grinning at the thought of Pete's harrowing night at the theater. Then, over the lodge, too quickly, then the dam, then into thickening clouds that were the final curtain on another summer at Arrowhead.

This same aerial view would repeat itself again and again until my last summer at the lake, the last before I met the woman I'd marry, graduated college, and went to Vietnam. I said more than once, "I'd never heard of Vietnam until I got off the plane," which wasn't really true but spoke to my insistence on living in the moment, not in the past or the future. Naturally, there would be rude awakenings.

Home from the lake, life returned to near normal. "How was your summer?" was difficult to answer. "I was on Mars," I'd say. Like Vietnam, I couldn't even try to explain it. You had to be there.

Dana came up for a fall weekend on campus. It was uncomfortable for both of us. She had little in common with my band of sarcastic, wry, cynical friends.

Oddly, that's what attracted me to her at the lake, where cynicism, sarcasm, and irony are almost nowhere to be found. Call it situational love. But don't quote me.

Dana was good-hearted and positive about almost all things. Life, for example. She always seemed to be in a good mood. Happy. For this, some thought her simple, easily amused.

She said she saw no point in obsessing about problems we weren't going to do anything about, except talk.

"How do you do it?" I asked. "How can you always be so happy?"

"I don't like to be unhappy," she said matter-of-factly.

I laughed. And laughed.

"What?" she asked.

"No one *likes* to be unhappy," I said, pointing out that it's a contradiction in terms. "It's not really a choice we make."

"We can try," she said.

* * *

We never saw each other again. Summer love. We no longer had much in common except memories. We'd spent the entire summer together, all our waking hours, working and playing in a dream world, where I always half expected to see Disney characters scurrying about.

Ed said not to worry: "Women are like streetcars, there's another one by every ten minutes." I'd heard him say that same thing to a girl except it was boys who were the streetcars.

I went back into social hibernation. I wouldn't call girls, then would get fixed up at the last minute with someone who was a leftover, like myself. While not great for the ego it was better than risking rejection by a girl in the semi-desirable range.

I continued to think that I deserved better, but there was no Uncle Ed around to get things started.

Yet! And yet! Somehow it happened, I met that girl I'd always had in mind, for years and years, even in sleep, which would make her the girl of my dreams, wouldn't it? We met at the last moment, the second semester of my second—yes it took me an extra one—senior year.

You won't be surprised to hear that she initiated it. I was

sitting on a stool in a campus bar guzzling beer when a tall, good-looking blonde approached with a cigarette between her fingers, struck a Lauren Bacall pose, and purred, "Got a light?"

What the hell was *this*? This kind of thing just didn't happen. Not to me.

"I love your work," she said.

What work? I did no work. My father couldn't get me to mow the lawn. My mom had stopped bothering to ask me to pick up my dirty socks.

"Your poems," she explained.

Now, attractive young women in the Midwest don't admire poetry. Girls with long stringy, dirty hair, skin like four miles of bad road, and B.O.—they're the ones who admire poetry. Not to mention my poems were nonsensical little nothings (although kind of funny, in my opinion). Unbeknownst to me they were being posted around campus.

The armadillo is an ugly thing,
Unlike the song bird it does not sing,
It won't do tricks in your yard,
It just lies around . . . and is hard.

"The Armadillo" by Bill Geist

Don't feel sorry for the leaves at all
Though they plunge from trees eighty feet tall

They'll return with the first breath of spring
The likes of us would die from such a thing.

"Why Weep for Leaves?" by Bill Geist

I eat chocolate sundaes with my friends
If a dollar they will lend
One night we ate three down at Joe's
We laughed ... and the chopped nuts came out my nose.

"Chocolate Sundaes" by Bill Geist

You can see why she fell so hard for me.

Her name was Jody. Our first date was to see Timothy Leary after which we did not drop LSD but rather drank beer at the Red Lion Inn. Very Midwestern.

That summer was my first away from Arrowhead in many years. I lived a block from Jody in Chicago. I landed a job pulling down $600 a month in the advertising department of Libby's food company on Michigan Avenue, where armies of workers walked fast, wore serious suits, and carried briefcases. I had no ties. Jody made me a couple that were bold, brightly colored, hallucinogenic, Jefferson Airplane-ish.

Since I was going into the army in a few months I was assigned odds-and-ends at work, i.e., tasks no one else wanted. One was accompanying the head of advertising on business lunches with people from ad agencies.

I told Uncle Ed and he said it sounded perfect for me. "Ad guys do nothing but drink," he said, "and you've been in training for years."

My besotted boss and I would return from lunch. He'd close his office door, lie down on his couch, and "take a nap." I had no office. I put my head down on my desk, which was in a large room amidst a swirling sea of desks.

The young woman who sat at the next desk tapped me on the shoulder and suggested this was not a career-enhancing look for me. She explained that her goal in life was to become an executive at the company, which sounded very old-fashioned. This was a time, 1968, to buck all things establishment, not to enlist in it. We were just up Michigan Avenue from the Hilton Hotel, site of the Democratic convention riots that summer.

"Why?" I asked. To me, this was a time for reading the *Whole Earth Catalog*, smoking dope, tie-dyeing shirts, wearing bell-bottoms, listening to "In-A-Gadda-Da-Vida," that sort of thing. "Why would you want to dedicate your life to selling canned corn?" I asked, sharply.

"I think it's high time women made their way in the business world and made some money for a change," she said. And maybe it was, but do you have to sit in an office selling niblets?

I was of the opinion that it was far nobler to aspire to be a loving, caring person than to join the pack of materialistic, money-grubbing weasels. "People who know the price of everything and the value of nothing," as my grandmother used to say. (By the way, looking back, I have to say my side in the culture war lost.)

Another of my tasks at Libby's was answering customer mail. My responses went something like this:

Dear Mrs. McGillicuddy,

We regret to learn that you found a thumb in a can of our French-cut green beans. Enclosed please find three 50-cents-off coupons on your next purchase of Libby's fine line of canned and frozen vegetables.

Very truly yours

Beats a $100 million lawsuit.

We were in Chicago and witnessed the Democratic convention riots. Believe it or not, that was the first time it really hit me that I was going to Vietnam.

Both Uncle Ed and my older brother, David, counseled me on military service. Ed thought a ground war in Asia was crazy and unwinnable, but figured I'd probably be drafted so should complete the ROTC program and at least I'd be an officer. My brother concurred. He was an army officer stationed in Germany and having a fine time. Elvis was there.

So, I stayed in ROTC, and consequently became *the only person I knew* who went to Vietnam.

My dad was in the hospital with heart problems when I left. Neither of us knew what to say. He said, "Hide behind a tree."

Uncle Ed pulled some strings with an old army buddy still serving and I was assigned to the Signal Corps (as Ed had been), which included all army photographers. I thought that being a photographer would allow me to approach my tour in Vietnam not so much as a killer but rather as something of a journalist.

I even volunteered to go to Vietnam six months early to ensure I'd get the photography job. But upon arrival I was assigned a job monitoring radio dials in the Delta. "What about the photography?" I yelled at the guy doling out the assignments. "Great hobby," he replied.

Uncle Ed hadn't forgotten me. It's just that these things take forever to go through channels. One day my commanding officer in the Delta called me in and said: "Well, you got your wish, you're going to the First Infantry Division as a combat photographer. God, I wish I was going with you." Career officers wanted to be in combat units (not radio dial watching), where they would rake in lots of medals and accompanying promotions.

A sign at the front gate read: "1st Infantry Division. No Mission Too Difficult—No Sacrifice Too Great—Duty First." A second sign read: "Welcome to Rocket City." Be careful what you wish for. I'd forgotten that to be a combat photographer I'd have to be in or near combat. It was a long year. Jody sent me cookies. My comrades-in-arms learned to identify the boxes and took to hacking them open with machetes. My mother-in-law sent me a sweater to keep me warm in the jungle. Pete from the lake sent me Yahtzee score pads for which I have not properly thanked him.

When I returned from Vietnam, Janet and Ed met me at my arrival gate, which you could do back in the good old days three decades before 9/11. When Ed saw me, he cried. I hadn't expected that. I'd always forced myself to be in a jovial mood when I was going to see him. I was the funny guy. It was and is my currency. But seeing him, I shed a tear too. I think the whole family was just happy they hadn't lost another William E. Geist to war.

I was stationed at Fort Riley, Kansas, but Jody married me anyway. When I found I could be discharged early if I went back to school, I applied immediately to the graduate program at the University of Missouri's School of Journalism. I was accepted despite my 3.1 undergraduate grade-point average, which doesn't sound all that bad, but it's on a 5.0 scale. Some concluded that Ed must have played a role in my admission. Could be. He'd been elected president of the Missouri Restaurant Association and had come to know a lot of bigwigs around the state.

After college I landed a job as a reporter at what was called the *Suburban Trib*, the "Little *Trib*," a *Trib*-let if you will, the lowest rung at the *Chicago Tribune*, covering sewer bond referenda, new left-turn lanes, and changes in school lunch menus. To boost morale I did things like putting clocks on the wall like they do at real newspapers labeled "New York," "London," and "Tokyo" except ours were labeled "Arlington Heights," "Hoffman Estates," and "Buffalo Grove": all suburbs.

When I next saw Uncle Ed at the lake, he introduced me as

"the editor of the *Chicago Tribune*," which was, oooh, a good twenty-five promotions away. He always erred on the plus-plus side. Bless him.

* * *

Arrowhead Lodge was gone. I knew that before I drove slowly up the long hill leading to the completely empty site two years ago. It had been purchased and torn down. I'd seen painful photographs of heavy demo equipment ripping it apart like lions tearing at an antelope carcass.

Truth be told, the Arrowhead Lodge I knew was gone long before the wrecking crews arrived. The beginning of the end began when employees had to punch in and out on a time clock. When waitresses and bellhops had to record their tips on tax forms. When a monstrous automatic dishwasher was installed. When there was talk of minimum wage laws. When the town of Lake Ozark was founded and local codes were enacted. When much of the fun and vitality disappeared because college kids stopped coming to work summers—perhaps because they could no longer make a dent in soaring college costs, or perhaps, as some have suggested, because American kids would really rather not work anymore. When a Holiday Inn ("No surprises") went up a quarter mile down the road.

Bizarre new decor at Arrowhead didn't help, God knows. In what appeared to be an act of desperation the new owner laid black and white tiles in a checkered pattern on the dining room floor, then installed a forest of heavy black wrought-iron street-lights. The overall effect was a bad acid trip in New Orleans.

And—here in the Ozarks—a glass elevator was installed from the front sidewalk to the Pow Wow Pub on the second floor. Arrivederci, charm.

The overriding problem was that the new highway to the lake somehow bypassed Arrowhead Lodge and practically the entire lake! Motorists would see the lake at seventy miles per hour and only as they crossed two bridges. It was a lot faster now to get to nowhere.

Ed and Janet had moved far away, to a penthouse in a new high-rise in North Palm Beach. Jody and I would fly down with the kids to see them and Ed would take us to some dark bar in a mall—not the kind of place folks trying to escape cold, dark, gray New York are looking for, especially those with kids. Willie and Libby played on the floor underneath the table. "Kids, don't eat the cigarette butts!" (Later, he did take us to lunch at a place with windows.)

Aunt Janet was a few years older than Ed and died before he did. She was cremated in Florida and we accompanied her ashes back to Illinois where they were buried in a family plot next to her parents and Uncle Bill.

Uncle Ed was carrying her ashes in a box as he boarded the plane. When he spotted a youngish blonde with an empty seat next to her, he stowed Janet's ashes in the overhead, sat down next to the blonde, and asked if he could buy her a drink.

Ed found new drinking buddies in Florida. One was the pastor of his Episcopal church. When we drove over to the parsonage, Ed opened his trunk and took out a half gallon of Dewar's.

Ed's mailman was another. I walked into his apartment and the two of them were sitting on the couch in the living room drinking scotch. The mailman, Jimmy, was in uniform, his bag at his feet. Ed asked him if he'd like another drink. "I can't stay too long," Jimmy replied, accepting a refill but still mindful of his sworn duty to the U.S. Postal Service. "Neither rain nor sleet nor hail, nor drunken stupor..." Despite their sizable age difference, the two became good friends as folks with a common interest so often do.

Ed suffered a stroke. And the pastor checked him into the hospital.

"Does Mr. Popkess drink alcohol?" asked the admitting nurse.

"Yes, he does," the pastor answered.

"How often? Once a week, twice a week, or more?"

"More," was the answer.

"How much would you estimate he consumes?"

"Let's see," said the pastor, "there's the drink around noon, then a couple at lunch. There's the five o'clock, then a couple before dinner and maybe one during the meal."

"How much then would you say he consumes daily?"

"Just under a fifth," the pastor calculated.

"Per week?"

"Day," the pastor answered.

There wasn't a box to check for that, so the nurse entered a notation in long hand in the margin.

"And how long has he had this habit? Six months? A year? More?"

"I'd say, oooh, probably fifty or sixty years," the pastor said. Wasn't a box for that either.

"Wow," said the nurse, somewhat unprofessionally and with a note of admiration.

Doctors prescribed a shot of scotch every day so that Uncle Ed's body would not go into shock.

I brought a get-well card to the hospital, a drink menu from his favorite bar in Palm Beach, Taboo, signed by all the waitresses.

He recovered enough to go out to lunch and it was then he uttered the last word I heard him say: "Scotch!" he yelled at an inattentive waitress who snapped to. Earlier he'd nearly taken off her hand at the wrist when she'd attempted to take his glass, which she viewed as empty but which he knew from vast experience still had a drop down there amongst the melting ice cubes. It wasn't frugality, he just regarded scotch as some sort of sacred nectar.

Ed passed away shortly thereafter at age eighty. I recalled him telling me: "When you bury me, pour some scotch on the grave—and don't let it pass through you first." We did.

On my last trip to the lake, I rented a boat and found the lake to be swarming with thousands of boats. You really needed rearview mirrors and turn signals. Some days, they say, it seems you could walk across the hulls from one side of the lake to the other. On the Fourth of July literally thousands of drunken sailors, or powerboaters rather, jam into Party Cove. Picture Mardi Gras with everyone on Bourbon Street driving a boat.

Some vessels are big enough these days to qualify as ocean-going: fifty-five feet or so. Pilots seem to purposely set their throttles for maximum wakes, creating four- or five-foot waves that swamp small craft and destroy docks. Boaters die here with some regularity. The cigarette-style boats are deafening and can easily outrun police boats—and helicopters. Top speed: 244 miles per hour.

Homes sit dock-to-dock for miles on Shawnee Bend where there were nearly none before the toll bridge There are some high-rise condos over there now and stoplights.

I strolled the large vacant expanse where Arrowhead once was, trolling for memories. But there was really nothing left to see, nothing identifiable, no reminders to tug at my heart-strings, to conjure all of those memories of summers long ago. Nothing but the barren emptiness.

Jim Chappell visits the sacred ruins of Arrowhead Lodge.

An arrowhead-shaped stone flower bed that had been just outside the front door was all that remained. The big arrowhead neon sign that rose twenty-five feet out of the flower bed was gone, replaced by a small "For Sale" sign.

I sat down on the stone flower bed. I felt numb. This was nowhere I'd been before. I guess that the passing of people and places we love, over time, loses some of its power to break our hearts. Take that, death.

I recalled thinking way back that this rustic old lodge made of rough-hewn local trees and stone was the only thing that looked like it really belonged here.

I remembered thinking that perhaps it would come back into vogue as vacationers tired of the chain motels and longed for something historic and real.

But the tide of souvenir shops, go-cart tracks, and mini-golf courses on the strip now flows all the way to the spot where Arrowhead Lodge once was. It had become what no longer belonged.

Postscript

*E*verything changed when I was dropped off at Arrowhead Lodge that first summer.

At home, I did nothing. I'd say "next to nothing" except "next to nothing," while very close indeed to nothing, is not close enough.

I rose late and the first thing I didn't do was make my bed. In a few hours, it would just be messed up again. What is gained?

Sometimes my mom would give up and make it herself. And since she was in there anyway, she picked up my dirty socks, washed them and hung them out to dry on a clothesline with clothespins. She ironed. She folded. She shopped, cooked, washed, and dried the dishes (with her dishpan hands).

At the lake I found myself suddenly and rather shockingly on my own. I had counted on freedom from home and parents being one of the very best aspects—besides beer—of spending the summer away. But what about all of these relentless, nagging chores? Day in and day out. Who washes the socks?

I always thought that the message you see on those join-the-army the posters, "Freedom Is Not Free," was just a recruiting gimmick. But, no. There is a price to pay for freedom.

My family said everything changed.

I took that to mean things like ironing, which I'd never done before. But they meant more important things, fundamental, life-changing things.

But first, about the ironing. I'd never touched an iron let alone tried to use one. As a bellhop I had to wear a starched, ironed, wrinkle-free white shirt *every day*. And, as mentioned earlier, we had to iron our own shirts *ourselves*!

One bit of good news: I was pleased to learn that starch was no longer boiled and stirred in big black iron vats like the settlers did. Or was that laundry?

Today, we have spray starch. But, as I learned through trial and error, you have to keep the iron moving. Linger for a split second and you leave a big ugly brown burn mark. The face of the iron resembled the shape of an arrowhead so when people remarked on the unsightly burn I would explain that it was the Arrowhead Lodge logo. (Not sure if we had logos back then. I think we did but didn't know they were called logos.)

Now, about those life changes.

My cousin Charlie, Janet's son, put it this way: "Arrowhead Lodge was the beginning of Billy Geist." He took my brother, David, and me nude water-skiing.

"Your parents were good parents, good people, they just didn't quite *get* you," my son, Willie, says.

In contrast to my quiet home life, Arrowhead was a lively, happy place, albeit with lots more hangovers. There was lots of laughter, most prominently Ed's distinctive booming: "Ha!-Ha!-Ha!"

And Janet and Ed *got* me. When I saw either one of them my brain would turn to the Amusing Things setting and I'd say something that would make them laugh or smile. Soon enough I was doing that with everyone. I became a Funny Person. People would start smiling when they ran into me. I liked bringing a smile. This was working out well.

I'd always been funny—hell, I was funny in *Bible* school— but I usually had to pay a price for it. Now, it was appreciated and rewarded.

It got to the point where I didn't need an audience. I'd think of funny things when no one was around and laugh inwardly. I could amuse myself.

I wrote down some of it. I remember writing a skit in high school for our senior class assembly, which included a bit about the amorous relationship between our red-haired and highly unpopular Dean of Boys and an Irish setter. I flopped on my bed when I wrote that and yelled inside my head: "*That* is funny!" That's the reward. Like the Aha! moment when that inventor guy said, "Come here, Watson. I think I've invented the telephone."

My red-haired grandmother, Nell, knew what time it was. She got me. She gave me a book of poetry. She'd marked the page with this poem by Ella Wheeler Wilcox:

Laugh, and the world laughs with you;
Weep, and you weep alone;
For this sad old earth must borrow its mirth,
But has trouble enough of its own.

"The lake gave you the confidence to run with it," Jody says.

That confidence led me to start writing humor, even after one teacher told me, loudly enough for the whole class to hear, "You're never going to get anywhere writing funny little stories." Next year, different teacher, I wrote a funny short story and got an A. To that point English class had largely meant diagramming sentences, which I had no interest in doing. Still don't diagram well.

Of course not everyone "got" it. I wrote kind of a New Journalism piece for a college feature-writing class on a colorful little barbecue shack ("We barbecue anything that walks, swims, or flies") where all sorts of people of all ages and backgrounds—black, white, cops, professors, high school coaches, kids—jammed into ten seats, mixed, talked, and dined together, probably the only place in town where this happened. My journalism instructor didn't like it. Said it wasn't really news. So, I wrote a drowsy three-part series on the diminishment of privacy in our society. A-plus.

The *Tribune* got it, eventually. The *New York Times* got it most days, although there were numerous skirmishes with editors early on. CBS got it, although at the outset there were a couple of producers who were pretty sure I was ruining the

Sunday Morning program. But the next thirty-one years went more smoothly.

As I learned from those entrepreneurs at the Lake of the Ozarks way back when, life is more difficult and rewarding and fun when you manage to do things your way. I think Frank Sinatra probably said this more eloquently and melodically.

Through my crazy poems, I met a beautiful woman whose most prized attribute in a man was his sense of humor. Her whole family felt that way. Her father was funny. Her mother was funny. Her siblings are funny.

And she maintains that the "Arrowhead Lodge Effect" continues. We had two children, Willie and Libby, both funny. They've given us four grandchildren: Lucie, George, Russell, and Billy. All funny as hell.

Acknowledgments

First and foremost, Uncle Ed and Aunt Janet, my second set of parents.

Jody, who throughout our forty-eight years together has never mounted a serious legal challenge to the "for better or worse" clause in our vows.

Our children, Willie and Libby, both talented, smart, thoughtful, accomplished, funny, and somehow humble. When the book sounded like a crabby old geezer from the mid-1900s (which I am), they told me so.

A multitude of the dearly departed who waited decades for me to find the time to write this book but finally threw in their towels.

My brain surgeons. If this book isn't all that you'd hoped, you can always reach them at home.

Tom Connor, my agent for nine books over nearly forty years.

Gretchen Young, my overly understanding, at times almost saintly, editor at Grand Central Publishing, her biblically patient colleague, Emily Rosman, and many others at GCP, to

193

include Ross McDonald, who designed this, my favorite of all my book covers.

Gina Chappell, former Arrowhead waitress, who with her husband, Jim, organized a reunion of former employees and shared her tales and photos.

All other former Arrowhead colleagues who also shared, to include Pete Havely, Tim (Wheezer) Short, and another Bill, who has to run for his public office and wisely requested his full name not be used.

Dwight Weaver, Lake of the Ozarks historian.

About the Author

Bill Geist is the *New York Times* bestselling author of nine books. He has won numerous Emmy Awards for his pieces on *CBS Sunday Morning*, as well as a star on the Hollywood Walk of Fame. Bill was awarded the Bronze Star for service as a combat photographer with the First Infantry Division in Vietnam in 1969.

He wrote a column on suburbia for the *Chicago Tribune* and the About New York column for the *New York Times* before joining CBS in 1987.

Bill has been married to Jody for more than forty-eight years. They have two children (Willie and Libby) and four grandchildren (Lucie, George, Russell, and Billy) and live in Riverside, Connecticut.